Red Books *showing the way*

LOCAL STREET ATLAS

G000021502

SOUTHAMPTON

BISHOPS WALTHAM · EASTLEIGH · HAMBLE-LE-RICE
HYTHE · ROMSEY · TOTTON · WICKHAM

CONTENTS

LEGEND

	Motorway
	Primary Route
	Other 'A' Road
	'B' Road
	Minor Road
	Pedestrianized / Restricted Access
	Track
	Built Up Area
	Footpath
	Stream
	River
Lock	Canal
	Railway / Station
●	Post Office
P P+	Car Park / Park & Ride
C	Public Convenience
✛	Place of Worship
→	One-way Street
i	Tourist Information Centre
8 8	Adjoining Pages
	Area Depicting Enlarged Centre
	Emergency Services
	Industrial Buildings
	Leisure Buildings
	Education Buildings
	Hotels etc.
	Retail Buildings
	General Buildings
	Woodland
	Orchard
	Recreational / Parkland
	Cemetery

Every effort has been made to verify the accuracy of information in this book but the publishers cannot accept responsibility for expense or loss caused by an error or omission.

Information that will be of assistance to the user of the maps will be welcomed.

The representation on these maps of a road, track or path is no evidence of the existence of a right of way.

Street plans prepared and published by
Red Books (Estate Publications) Ltd, Bridewell House, Tenterden, Kent, TN30 6EP.
The Publishers acknowledge the co-operation of the local authorities of towns represented in this atlas.

 Ordnance Survey® This product includes mapping data licensed from Ordnance Survey® with the permission of the Controller of Her Majesty's Stationery Office.

www.redbooks-maps.co.uk

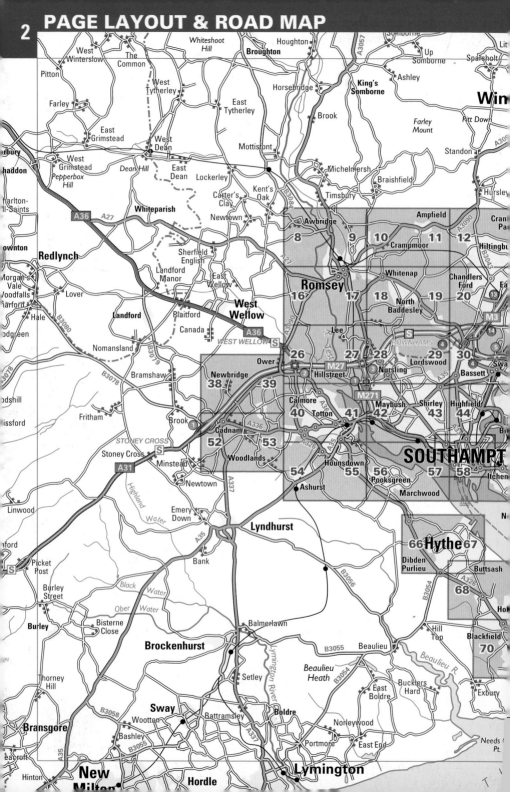

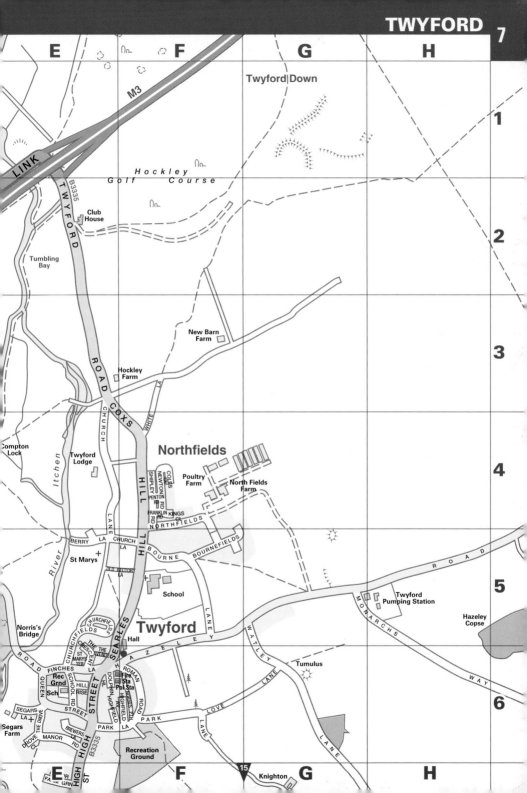

A B C D

8

DUNBRIDGE LA
B3084
Test Way

Awbridge

1

STANBRIDGE

Village Hall

The White House

Upper Ratley

LANE COOKS

LANE

Parsonage Farm

Rockwood Copse

2

Lower Ratley

COOMBE

Hilberry Farm

Stanbridge Earls

Sch

LANE

OLD SALISBURY

Rockwood Cottages

Lone Barn Farm

Test Way

3

SALISBURY

LANE OLD SALISBURY

OLD

Roke Manor Farm

SALISBURY

Grave Pit

Palmers Copse

4

Ranvilles n

Roke Manor

5

Squabb   Wood

Monks Cottages

Mead Mill Farm

Mill Race

Test Mill

Burnt Mill

MILL

MILLSTREAM RISE

Mill Stream

6

SALISBURY RD

A27

Springolt Farm

16

A B C D

A   **B**   **C**   **D**

Farm

1

Crookhill Farm

Sir Harold Hillier Gardens & Aboretum

Jermyns House

2

LANE

SANDY LA

BRAISHFIELD ROAD

JERMYNS

LANE

Bracken Wood

Outwood Lodge

Cemy

9

THE STRAIGHT MILE

South Copse

3

Ganger Common

Ganger Farm

South Holme Copse

WOODLEY

WOODLEY LANE

GANGER FARM ROAD

HORSESHOE

Woodley

Ganger Wood

Fish Farm

4

Sch

Hunters Inn

A3090

Crampmoor Farm

Oxlease Copse

GROVELY

CRAMPMOOR LA

Crampmoor

9

CEDAR LAWN

ROAD WINCHESTER ROAD

CRAMPMOOR

Ford

LANE

5

Harefield

Tadburn Lake

Halterworth Farm

Stroud School

Emer Farm

ST BLAIZE

JENNER

FELTHAM CL

WYNE

HIGHWOOD

HALTERWORTH

GREEN LANE

SEWARD RISE

HIGHWOOD LANE

6

Halterworth Lodge

HIGH FIRS

SAXON

KENNETH CL

Halterworth

BENEDICT CL

Warren Farm

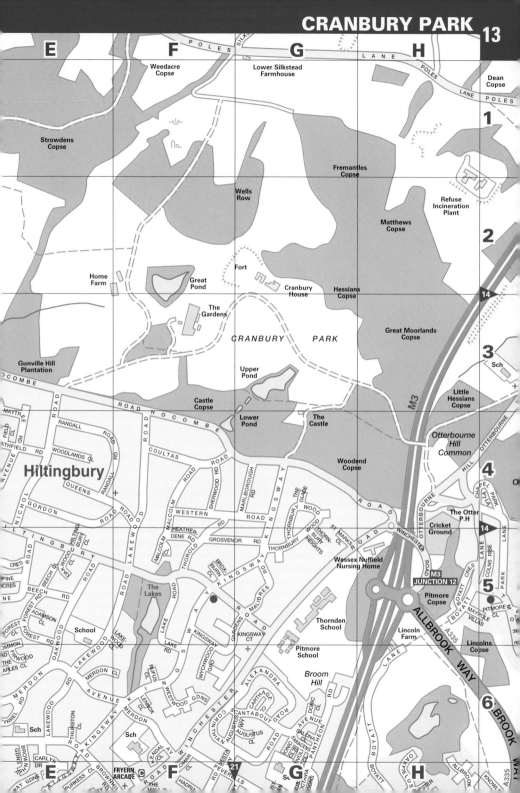

A **B** **C** **D**

1

2

3

4

5

6

South Down

Dean Copse

POLES LANE

M3

Refuse Incineration Plant

13

SPARROWGR

WATERWORKS

RICHMOND PK

HIGHWAYS RD

CROSSWAYS

GROVE RD

FAIRFIELD RD

SOUTHDOWN RD

SOUTHDOWN RD

ROAD

Itchen Way

River Itchen

Lock (dis)

Lock (dis)

Weir

Bore Holes

COPSE CT

NORLANDS DR

POLESBOURNE

OTTERBOURNE ROAD

OAKWOOD CL

REGENT CL

OAKWOOD AV

MEADOWCROFT CL

BROOKLYN CL

GREENACRES DR

Water Works

OLD PARSONAGE CT

DRIVE

MEDE

COLES

CRANBURY CL

MEWS CT

MAIN RD

CRANBOURNE

Otterbourne

CRAN-BOURNE DR

ZOTTERBOURNE HOUSE GDNS

Sch

Little Hessians Copse

Otterbourne Hill Common

Dell Copse

HILL

KILN LANE

KILN LANE

Otterbourne Farm

Cemy

Lock (dis)

Rosemary Leet

Stubbington R

OTTERBOURNE HILL

CHAPEL LANE

PARK LANE

Manor House

Moat

Kingfisher Stream

THE CLOSE

Brambridge House

Brambridge Park

COP DE

MO

Caravan Park

SPRING

The Otter P.H

13

ket und

Otterbourne Park Wood

LINCOLNS RISE

PITMORE LA

PARK LA

The Gardens

THE AVENUE

LANE

BOYATT CRES

BOYATT VILLAS

MAYROLE CL

PIT

Otterbourne Grange

LANE

Bugle Farm

CHURCH

Brambridge

UPPER MOORS

GRA CL LA

BISHOPSTO

Uppe Brambri Farm

Lincolns Copse

The Itchen Navigation

ON 12

ore se

A335

ALLBROOK WAY

ALLBROOK WAY

ROAD

Sch

Itchen Way

HIGHBRIDGE

WARDLE

LORDSWOOD ROAD

Hills Farm

High Bridge

Highbridge

ALLBROOK

KNOWL

PITMORE RD

Allbrook Farm

B3335 RD

22

Highbridge Farm

A335

E   F   A   G   H

Recreation Ground

7

Knighton

Cockscomb Hill Farm

1

Cockscomb Hill Copse

MANOR

DROVE

HIGH ST

B3335

MANOR FARM GRN

ROAD

HARE

HIGH ST

Gabriel's Copse

WATLEY LANE

LANE

2

fords ors

ROAD

MAIN

WOODLAND

LANE

DROVE

Park Farm

LANE

LANE

WATLEY

3

GHBRIDGE ROAD

MAIN

Colden Covert

Taylors Copse

Park Copse

Hensting Farm

4

ROAD

Rec Grnd

ORCHARD

NEW

SPRINGFIELDS CL

CHESTNUT AV

FRAMPTON CL

 SHOW

RING

LANE

SPRING HOUSE

BOYES LANE

Colden Common

Chalk Dell Copse

Kings Copse

Elm Farm

5

VIGOR

HAZEL CL

HILL LA

ASH

Caravan Park

BIRCH CL

WAY

ST

LIME

LANE

Caravan Park

SCOTTS

Strattons Copse

Inleys Copse

Bears Copse

Kennel Farm

CROWDERS GRN

BURR CL

CLAMP GRN

SETTERS

WHITEBEAM

ALDER CL

VEARS

VIGOR

ASPEN

Moreland's Copse

school

BRICKMAKR

THACKING GRN

CALLOWING GRN

PIPING GRN

PIPING

PIPING CL

EY CL

HACK DR

KILN GRN

NEARS LA

HAW-THORN CL

WILLOW GRN

WESSEX WY

BLACK GRN

Blacknells Copse

THOMPSONS

Swift's Farm

6

HURCH

NOBS

ROAD

MAIN

BRAMBLES CL

Nobs Crook

CROOK

HENSTING LANE

LANE

Colden Common Copse

S

CROOK 23

MAIN ROAD

B3354

E   F   G   H

Baddesley Common

Lights Copse

1

Castlehill Farm

Tredgo Cops

Ryders Farm

Manor House

Manor Farm

ROAD POUND LANE

FLEXFORD

ROAD

YEWBER WY

NEW

2

TEST VALLEY BUSINESS PARK

Alpine Lodge

MILE RIDE

20

Nutburn

BOTLEY ROAD

MIDDLE

MERRY

CAMELLIA LABURN UM CL

SIX OAKS RD

STREET END

NUTBURN RD

SANDY LA

Great Covert

3

St Johns Centre

EDWINA CL

WILLIS FLEMING

Rec Grnd

SANDY LA

CASTLE

Works

CHURCH CL

THE VINEYARDS

The Precinct

Schools

BROWNHILL

AVENUE ROAD

NORTON WELCH

FLEMING CL

Wrens Farm

Wrens Copse

Hogtrough Wood

LANE CASTL

4

THOMAS RD CL

FLEMING ROAD

HEATH RD

TANNERS RD

BRACKEN CL

MEADOW

Brown Hill

Health Centre Hall

Misslebrook Copse

MISSLEBROOK

Castle Lane Farm

20

BRACKEN CL

Club House

North Baddesley

CHILWORTH ROAD

Austins Copse

5

OLD

Chilworth Golf Course

Chilworth Old Village

FOWLERS WK

Spring Copse

WOODSIDE

Calveslease Copse

Manor Farm

VILLAGE

The Clump

WOODSIDE

ROAD

WOODSIDE

6

PARKWAY

CHILWORTH CL

WOODSID

Cricket Ground

hil A27

CHILW

Buxey Wood

Chilworth Manor

UNIVERSITY

MANOR ROAD

ORCHARD

Rownhams Plantation

Home Copse

E   F   G   H

29

UNIVERSITY ENT

PARKWAY

MAN

Allbrook

Highbridge

Lords Wood

Stoke Common

Bishopstoke

EASTLEIGH

BARTON PARK INDUSTRIAL ESTATE

THE TOWER INDUSTRIAL ESTATE

SHAKESPEARE BUSINESS PARK

Bishopstoke Playing Fields

Grid references: A B C D, rows 1–6

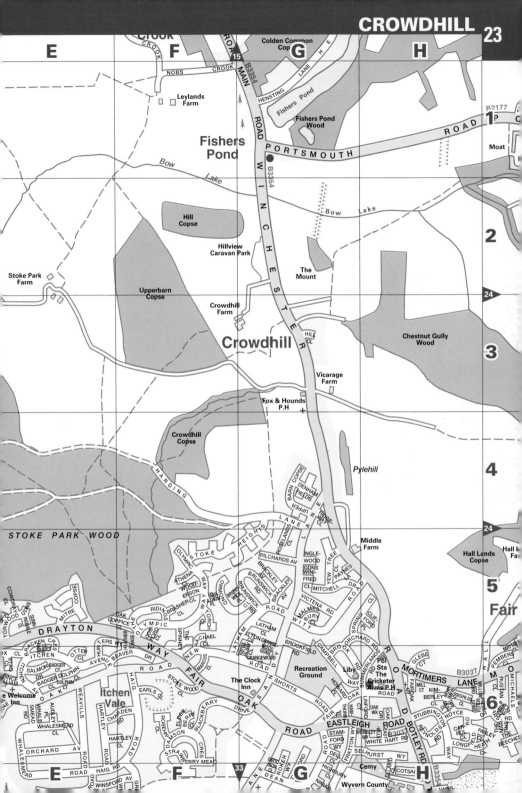

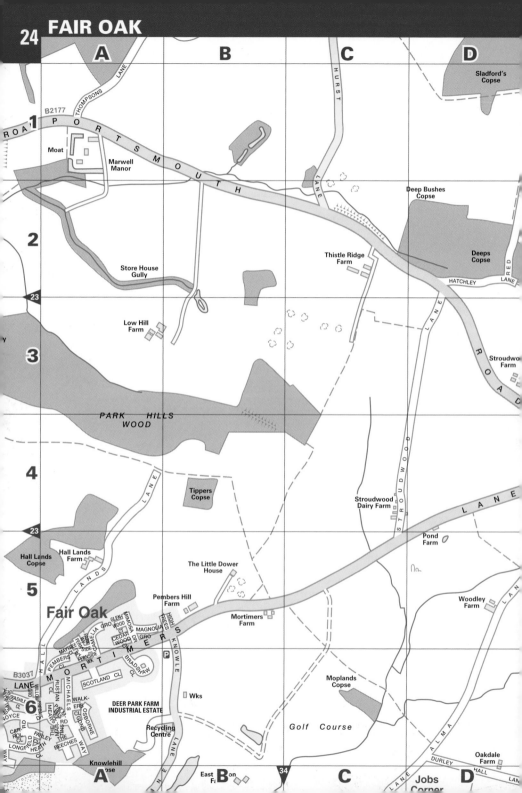

A   B   C   D

1

B2177

ROAD

THOMPSONS LANE

PORTSMOUTH

HURST LANE

Moat

Marwell Manor

Sladford's Copse

Deep Bushes Copse

2

Store House Gully

Thistle Ridge Farm

Deeps Copse

HATCHLEY

RED LANE

23

3

Low Hill Farm

STROUDWOOD ROAD

Stroudwood Farm

PARK HILLS WOOD

4

LANE

Tippers Copse

STROUDWOOD

Stroudwood Dairy Farm

LANE

23

5

Hall Lands Copse

Hall Lands Farm

LANDS

The Little Dower House

Pembers Hill Farm

HIGH TREES

KNOWLE

Mortimers Farm

Pond Farm

Woodley Farm

LANE

Fair Oak

MIMOSA WOOD

GLEN

GRO

CEDAR WOOD

MAGNOLIA GRO

CAMELLIA GRO

MORTIMERS

HALL LANE

PEMBERS

MATHER

SIDE WK

FERNSIDE

BRADSHAW

SCOTLAND CL

B3037

LANE

MICHAELS

RUSTAN RD

OSBORNE

WALK-ERS

GUNS

CL

6

WILLOW

NOYCE

MEAD

RD

THE BEECHES

WAY

FARLEY

HEATH

LONGFIELD

Scotland CL

DEER PARK FARM INDUSTRIAL ESTATE

Wks

Recycling Centre

Moplands Copse

Golf Course

ALMA LANE

Knowlehill Copse

A

East Fi on

B

34

C

DURLEY

HALL LANE

Oakdale Farm

D

Jobs Corner

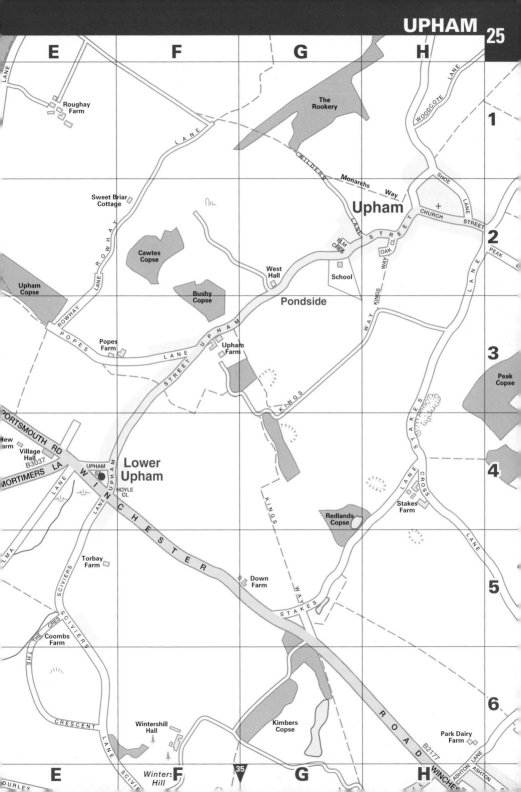

E F G H

1

Roughay Farm

WOODCOTE LANE

LANE

SHOE LANE

The Rookery

Monarchs Way

Upham

Sweet Briar Cottage

LANE

WILDERS LANE

CHURCH STREET

2

PEAK LANE

ELM CRES

ROWHAY LANE

Cawtes Copse

West Hall

STREET

OAK CL

KINGS WAY

School

Pondside

Upham Copse

Bushy Copse

ROWHAY

POPES

Popes Farm

LANE

UPHAM

Upham Farm

STREET

KINGS

3

Peak Copse

STAKES LANE

New Farm

PORTSMOUTH RD

Village Hall

B3037

MORTIMERS LA

Lower Upham

UPHAM ST

HOYLE CL

WINCHESTER

LANE UPHAM

KINGS

CROSS LANE

Stakes Farm

4

LMA

LANE

Torbay Farm

Redlands Copse

Down Farm

STAKES

5

SCIVIERS

THE CRES

Coombs Farm

THE

LANE

CRESCENT

SCIVIERS LANE

Wintershill Hall

Winters Hill

35

WAY

Kimbers Copse

ROAD WINCHE

B2177

Park Dairy Farm

ASHTON LANE ASHTON

6

E F G H

DURLEY

A   **B**   **C**   **D**

Romsey Common Farm

Brick Hill Farm

Grandmothers Copse

LA

16

Ridge Farm

Ridge

Ridge Copse

1

A3090

Moorcourt Copse

Shelley Nursery

2

A3090

Bowmans Farm

Busheylease Copse

A36

P

Blackwater Bridge

Busheylease Farm

Moat

Fish Ponds

Gravel Pit (dis)

Hotel

3

A36

River Blackwater

Wade Bridge

Moorcourt

RIDGE

STREET LANE

Cheneys Farm

Ower Bridge

River Cadnam

Wade Hill Farm

Wade Bridge

ROAD

WADE HILL DROVE

4

M27 JUNCTION 2

M27

HILL

Wade Park Farm

39

Depot

Hillstreet

Colbury House

SALISBURY RD

Drove Hill Wade

The Laurels Farm

5

Golden Gutter

Brookes Hill

Hattons Plantation

Green Lane Farm

STREET

Shavershill Plantation

SALISBURY RD

TOTTON WESTERN BY-PASS

SALISBURY

Brookes Wood

LOPERWOOD

Calmore Croft Farm

GREEN LA

6

Gipsies Fir Plantation

A326

Croft Farm

PAULETTS LANE

ROAD SA

Sharves Hill

A36

Testwood Lakes

Testwood House

wyford

Shornhill Great

LANE LOPE

Paulets Row

B

40

Calmore

C

Kilnyard Copse

Little Testwood

A   **B**   **C**   **D**

E F 17 G H

Footbridge

Lee Park Farm

Skidmore

Longbridge Farm

LEE CHURCH LANE

Aqueduct

Lee Manor Farm

Lee

Test Way

River Test

CHURCH LANE

LEE

Canal Pio

COLDHARBOUR

Longbridge Lake

1

ROMSEY ROAD

2

LANE

Grove Farm

28

Fir Copse

3 Upt

The Atherley School

Casa Aquila Farm

Griffon House

M271

Gravel Works

LEE LANE

CHURCH LANE

Manor Farm

CHURCH LANE

UPTON

LANE

4 ON

M27 JUNCTION 3

M27

Nursling House

UPTON

STATION RD

28 NURS

Broadlands Lake

Electricity Sub Sta

DAIRY

LANE

ORIANA

Nu

5

Gravel Tip

STATION LANE

CANBERRA

ROAD

MAURETANIA

NURSLING INDUSTRIAL ESTATE

MAJESTIC RD

MAJESTIC ROAD

6

Conagar Bridge

MILL

Nursling Mill

Trout Farm

Manor House Farm

River Test

WESTON LANE

ROAD

FRANK DR

Superstore

Blackwater

ver

E F 41 G H

E · F · 19 · G · H

Home Copse · Chilworth Manor · Cricket nd

wnhams antation

Long Copse · Kennels Farm · Satellite Station · Chilworth Common · **1**

UNIVERSITY · PARKWAY · ENTERPRISE · VENTURE RD · MANOR ROAD · ROMAN ROAD

Hazel Copse · SCIENCE & RESEARCH CENTRE

M27

Matthews Moor · DROVE · M27 JUNCTION 4 · **30**

Chilworth Tower · CHILWORTH · LORDSWOOD LANE · Chilworth Common · **2**

Dymers Wood

Tanners Brook

ROM · THE NG · Chilwo Ring · **3**

L O R D S · W O O D

Clams Copse

Castle Hill · Redlodge Belt · Pr Gol · GOLF · Club House · **4**

Ford · Whinchae · BRAM BLING CL · WIDGEON CL · WARBLER ROAD · TINTAGEL · DUNVEGAN · **30**

WRYNECK · HAWFINCH · SANDPIPER · FIRECREST · SHELDRAKE GDNS · PUFFIN · BALMORAL CL · DUNSTER CL · MELVILLE DRIVE

KESTREL · PLOVER · Sch First School · FULMAR · CURLEW CL · OSPREY · GRAFTON GDNS · Hockey Grnds · Ski Slope · **5**

KING SID · GOLDCREST GDNS · TURNSTONE GDNS · OAKWOOD · PRUNUS CL · GREEN · ABBOTS FIELD · Cricket Ground · Football Ground · Athletics & Cycle Track · Red Lodge

therland School

HOLI HOLI

Municipal Golf Course

BTHOLT CL · LORDS · BEAULIEU CL · PETWORTH GDNS · LONGLEAT GDNS · COWDRAY CL · WOBURN · ROBINIA · SALERNO · TARANTO · Cricket Ground · CIVIC SPORTS CENTRE · All Weather Pitches · Cricket Grounds · Red L Seconda

NISTOR CL · THOLT CL · CROYDON CL · GATWICK DRIVE · ROWNHAMS · GAMBLE · SILVAN · ABERD · DRIVE · WALTHAM · BRANS · BURF · CRES · PURB · CL · LORDS · WOOD · Red Lo

Lords Hill · LANG · BLAKE · IRISH RD · SHALDEN · Health Centre · DUNKIRK · CURZON CL · Pub In The Park · REDHILL CL · REDHILL CRES

LINDEN · PEACH RD · HOLLY OAK RD · OUTER · ROAD · SPRING FORD CL · SPRINGFORD · GREYWELL AV · BURN RD · WONSTON · PRESHAW · AV · ARNHEM · ARNHEM RD · DUNKIRK RD · LIME · THORNHILL GDNS · HIGHCLERE RD · ABINGD · FERNLEA · POINTOUT ·

CIRCLE · Hollybrook Cemetery · **Lordswood** · CRESFORD · COXFORD · SEAC · GARTH · Pub In The Park · DREWOOD ·

6

WINCHES

E · **Aldermoor** · F · 43 · Hollybrook Cemetery · Maternity · G · H · Hall · CHESTER RD

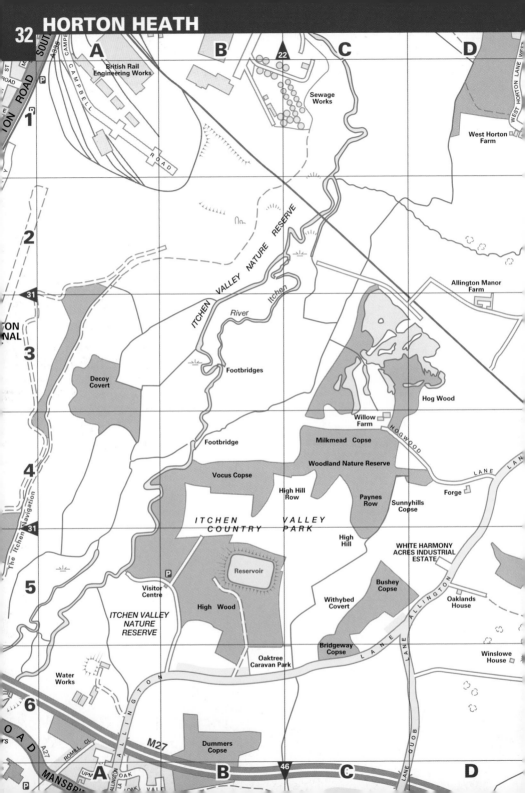

A B 22 C D

SOUT

CAMPE

ST
ROAD

ON ROAD
A335

CAMPBELL
ROAD

1

British Rail
Engineering Works

Sewage
Works

West Horton
Farm

WEST HORTON LANE WES

2

ITCHEN VALLEY NATURE RESERVE

Itchen

31

River

Allington Manor
Farm

ON
NAL

3

Decoy
Covert

Footbridges

Hog Wood

Willow
Farm

HOGWOOD

Footbridge

Milkmead Copse

Woodland Nature Reserve

LANE LANE

4

Vocus Copse

High Hill
Row

Paynes
Row

Sunnyhills
Copse

Forge

The Itchen Navigation

31

ITCHEN
COUNTRY

VALLEY
PARK

High
Hill

WHITE HARMONY
ACRES INDUSTRIAL
ESTATE

5

Visitor
Centre

Reservoir

Withybed
Covert

Bushey
Copse

ALLINGTON

Oaklands
House

ITCHEN VALLEY
NATURE
RESERVE

High Wood

Bridgeway
Copse

LANE

LANE

Winslowe
House

Water
Works

Oaktree
Caravan Park

ALLINGTON

6

ROMILL CL

A27

M27

ALLINGTON

QUOB

LANE

MANSBRI

OAK VALE

Dummers
Copse

UPM

A B 46 C D

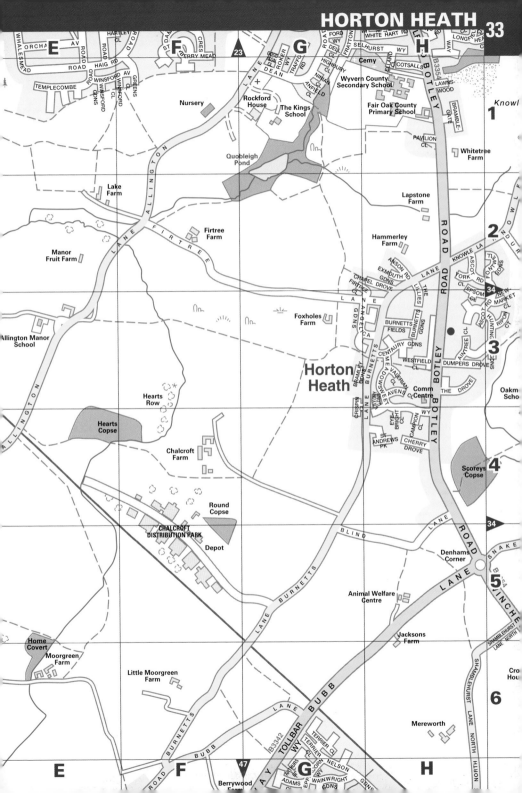

A **B** **C** **D**

Knowehill Copse

East Horton Farm

Jobs Corner

Oakdale Farm

BEECHES WAY

DURLEY HALL LANE

BRAMBLE GATE

Knowle Hill

Knowle Hill Farm

1

Whitetree Farm

Durley Copse

Greenwood Manor

KNOWLE LANE

Copperbeech Farm

GREENWOOD

KNOWLE LA
ASCOT RD
FONTWELL CL
NEWBOLTS

The Cockpit Farm

2

Greenwood

YORK CL
33
NEW-MARKET
RIPON CT
HUNTINGDON GDNS

ROAD

GREENWOOD LANE

AINTREE CL
EMPERS DROVE
DROVE

Oakmore School

3

Berkeley Farm

CHURCH LANE

Church Croft Farm

BROOK

ROAD

Durley

Sch Copse

Sc

4

Beech Corner

DURLEY LANE

Sch

Lower Farm

PARSONAGE LANE

Durley

ROAD

33

SNAKEMOOR LANE

Snakemoor Farm

STAPLEFORD LANE

Little Snakemoor Farm

WHITEGATES LANE
KYTES LANE
THE SAWMILLS
STREET
GREGORY

hams rner

B3354

5

WINCHESTER

Stapleford Farmhouse

HEATHEN LANE

SHAMBLEHURST LANE NORTH

Croft House

6

Blundells Copse

SHAMBLEHURST LANE NORTH

ROAD

B3354

CHANCELLORS

Ford

Hill Farm

A **B** **C** **D**

24

48

Wintershill

Durley Street

Winters Hill

Durley Hall Farm

Nursery

Newto

Albany

WINCHESTER RD

ASHTON LANE
ASHTON CLOSE

Farm

Tangier Farm

Elm Tree Farm

Durley Manor Farm

Middle Farm

Broom Farm

Mincingfield Farm

Park Lug

Brownheath Park

Brown Heath

MINCINGFIELD TER

Brokes Copse

Channels Farm

Treefiel Farm

River Hamble

Brokes Farm

Maple Farm

Calcot House

Calcot Farm

CALCOT LANE

MILL LA

BOTLEY ROAD

B3035

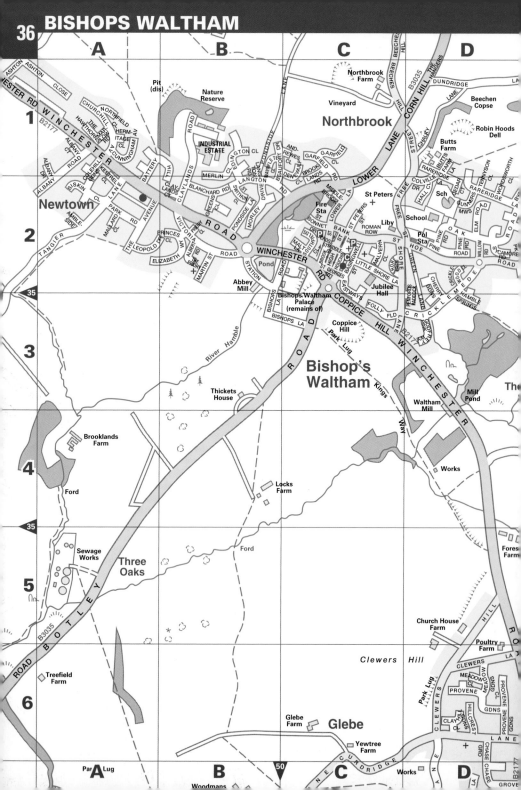

A   **B**   **C**   **D**

1

2

35

3

4

35

5

6

Northbrook Farm
Vineyard
Northbrook
Beechen Copse
Robin Hoods Dell
Butts Farm
Nature Reserve
Pit (dis)
INDUSTRIAL ESTATE
St Peters
School
Liby
Pol Sta
Fire Sta
Roman Row
Little Shore La
Malvern
Jubilee Hall
Abbey Mill
Bishops Waltham Palace (remains of)
Coppice Hill
Park Lug
Newtown
Pond
River Hamble
Thickets House
Bishop's Waltham
Kings Way
Waltham Mill
Mill Pond
The
Brooklands Farm
Ford
Works
Fores Farm
Sewage Works
Three Oaks
Ford
Locks Farm
Church House Farm
Poultry Farm
Clewers Hill
Park Lug
Treefield Farm
Glebe Farm
Glebe
Yewtree Farm
Works
Woodmans
Par Lug

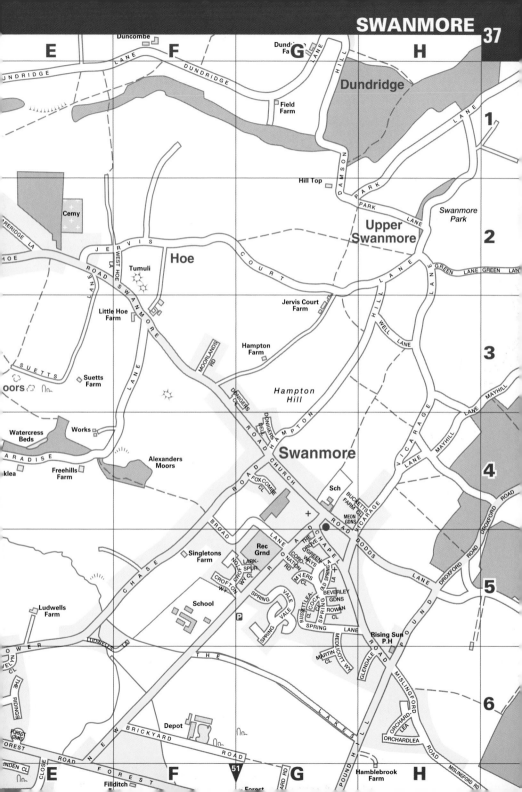

E   F   G   H

Duncombe

Dund... Fa   **Dundridge**

DUNDRIDGE

Field Farm

1

Hill Top

Cemy

Upper Swanmore

Swanmore Park

JERVIS LA

WEST HOE LANE

Hoe

COURT

Tumuli

GREEN LANE   GREEN LAN

2

Little Hoe Farm

Jervis Court Farm

Hampton Farm

HILL LANE

WELL LANE

3

SUETTS

Suetts Farm

oors

Hampton Farm

MOORLANDS RD

Hampton Hill

HAMPTON

VICARAGE LANE

MAYHILL LANE   MAYHILL

Watercress Beds

Works

DENGERS CL

BELL ROAD

DROXFORD   ROAD

4

ARADISE

Freehills Farm

DENGERS RD

CHURCH ROAD

Swanmore

Sch   BUCKETTS FARM

VICARAGE LA

klea

Alexanders Moors

BROAD ROAD

FOXCOMBE CL

MEON GDNS

X

DODDS LANE

DROXFORD ROAD

5

Singletons Farm

LANE

Rec Grnd

A TRE DR GREEN CORO WAYS

CHAPEL ROAD

OLD SPRING LA

BEVERLEY GDNS

POUND LANE

CHASE

NO CRO CL

LARK-SPUR CL

MYERS CL

DI NATION RD

RUSS KETTLE LA

COCK

OLD SPRING

ROWAN CL

School

CROFTON WY

SPRING VALE

SPRING VALE

SPRING LANE

Rising Sun P.H

MEDICOTT WY

GLENDALE ROAD

MISLINGFORD

6

Ludwells Farm

OWER

THE RIDINGS

LUDWELLS LA

THE

MARTIN CL

ORCHARD LEA

ORCHARDLEA

FOREST GDNS

INDEN CL

THE

Depot

NEW BRICKYARD ROAD

CLOSE ROAD FOREST

FOREST

Hamblebrook Farm

MISLINGFORD RD

E   F   **51**   G   H

Fillditch

Forest

A **B** **C** **D**

1

Furzley

Half Moon
Common

Court
Copse

Warren Hill

Furzley
Common

2

Duck Hill

Fuzzies
Copse

Stagbury Hill

Newbridge
Farm

Tumulus

3

Crock Hill

Cadnam
Bog

Newbridge

Newbridge
Inclosure

4

Cadnam Common

Bunk

Storms
Farm

Robins Brook
Farm

Coppittho
Hill

5

KEWLAKE

Withers
Farm

Pollar
Moor Fa

Manor
Farm

Springers
Farm

Cadnam
Green

Pollards
Moor

6

Biddlecombe
Farm

The Marsh
Farm

WITTENSFORD LANE

KEWLAKE LA

CADNAM LANE

M27

ROMSEY ROAD

NEWBRIDGE ROAD

POLLARD

52

A **B** **C** **D**

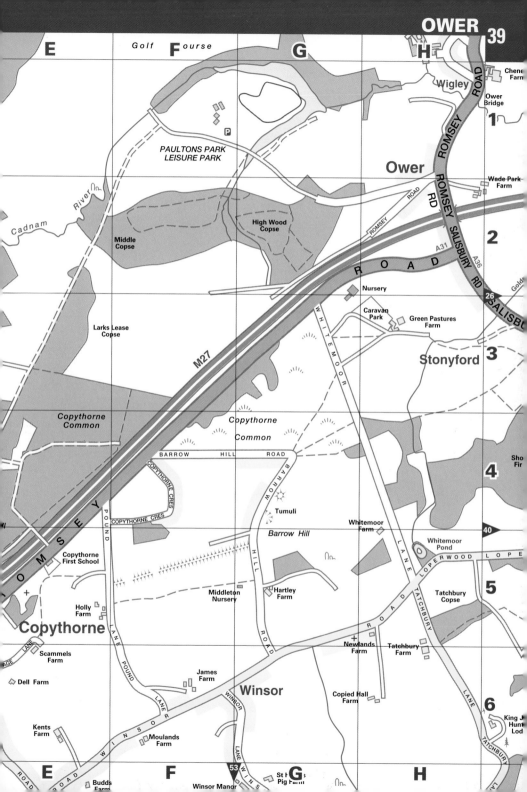

E   F   G   H

Golf Fourse

Wigley

Chene
Farm

Ower
Bridge

1

PAULTONS PARK
LEISURE PARK

P

Ower

ROMSEY ROAD

Wade Park
Farm

High Wood
Copse

ROMSEY RD.

ROMSEY

RD

SALISBURY RD.

A36

A31

River

Cadnam

Middle
Copse

ROAD

2

Nursery

Caravan
Park

Green Pastures
Farm

A36

26

SALISBU

Gold

Larks Lease
Copse

M27

Stonyford

3

Sho
Fir

Copythorne
Common

Copythorne

Common

WHITEMOOR

4

BARROW   HILL   ROAD

COPYTHORNE CRES

COPYTHORNE CRES

BARROW

40

ROMSEY

POUND

Tumuli

Barrow Hill

Whitemoor
Farm

Whitemoor
Pond

LOPERWOOD   LOPE

Copythorne
First School

HILL

Middleton
Nursery

Hartley
Farm

LANE

TATCHBURY

ROAD

Tatchbury
Copse

5

Copythorne

Holly
Farm

LANE

POUND

ROAD

Newlands
Farm

Tatchbury
Farm

LANE

Scammels
Farm

LANE

James
Farm

Dell Farm

WINSOR

Winsor

Copied Hall
Farm

TATCHBURY

6

King J
Hunt
Lod

Kents
Farm

WINSOR LANE

ROAD

Moulands
Farm

St
Pig Farm

LANE   WINS

53

Winsor Manor

Budds
Farm

E   F   G   H

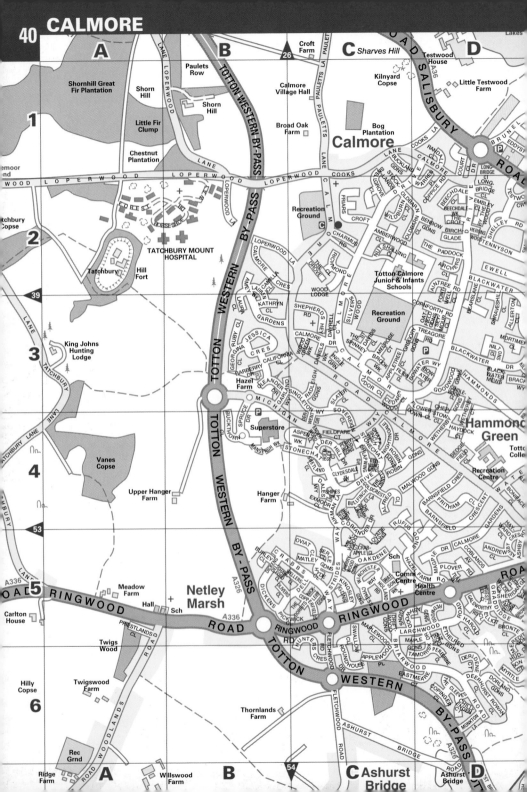

E F G H

1

2

3

4

5

6

27

42

42

55

Superstore

TEST VALLEY BUSINESS CENTRE

MAN D PARK
YEOMAN PK

GOVER
WESTOVER

Anchor Hotel
Red Bridge

Footbridge

Pumping Station

Chadney Meadow

Ruddy Mead

Yarnsey

River Test

GRIFFIN INDUSTRIAL PARK

LULWORTH BUSINESS PARK

SOUTH HAMPSHIRE INDUSTRIAL PARK

Testwood

Salmon Leap

Lower Test Nature Reserve

Test Way

SALISBURY

Playing Field

School

The Furlongs Nature Reserve

Recreation Ground

Sch

A36

Totton
Sch

COMMERCIAL ROAD

REDBRIDGE CAUSE

Health Centre
Fire Sta
Civic Centre
Amb Sta
Liby
Library
SALISBURY ROAD ARCADE

Supermarket

ROAD

HIGH STREET

Works

TOTTON

Eling Great Marsh

Eling Wharf

RINGWOOD ROAD RINGWOOD

A336

Brokenford

Sports Ground

Abbotswood School

Sch

MAYNARD ROAD

BY PASS

RUMBRIDGE

Depot

Sch

East Quay

Works

Rushington

Rum Bridge
Recreation Ground

MARCHWOOD BY-PASS

HILL SPICERS HILL

Mus
Tide Mill
Toll Bridge

Eling Hill

Cemy

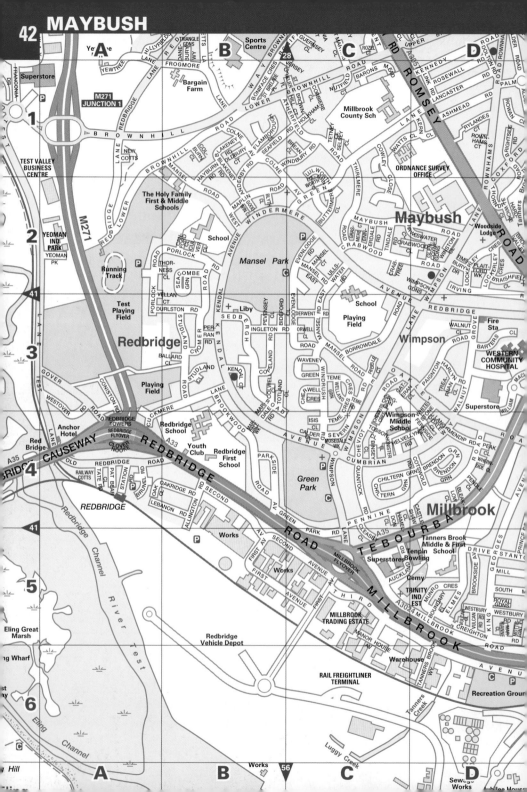

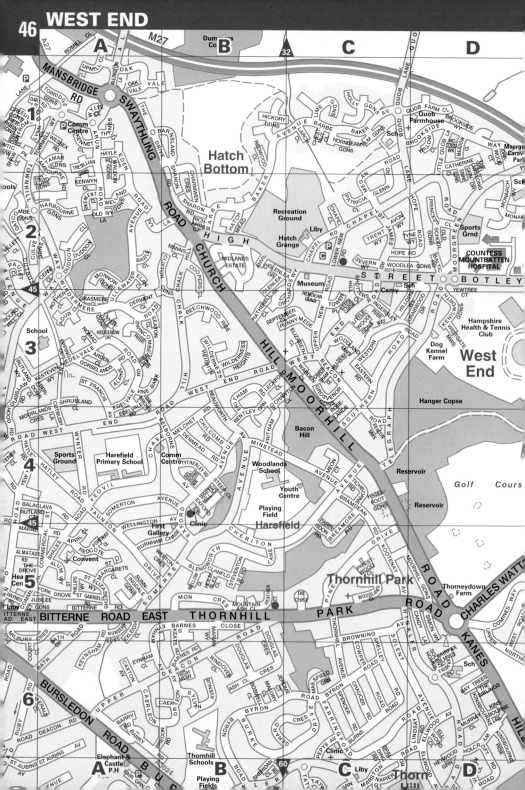

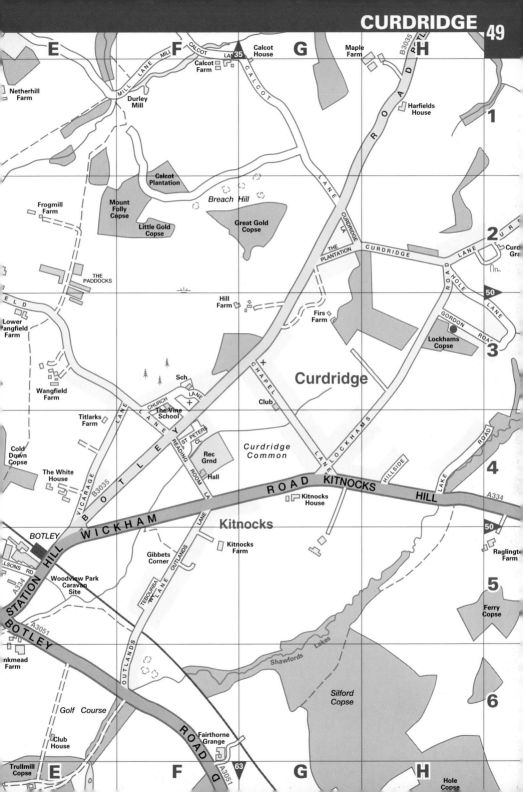

E F G H

Netherhill Farm

MILL LANE

MILL LANE

CALCOT LANE

Calcot Farm

Calcot House

B3035 PTL

Maple Farm

35

Harfields House

1

Durley Mill

CALCOT LANE

Calcot Plantation

Breach Hill

Great Gold Copse

CURDRIDGE LA

CURDRIDGE

ROAD

2

Frogmill Farm

Mount Folly Copse

Little Gold Copse

THE PLANTATION

CURDRIDGE LA

LANE

HOLE LANE

Curd Gra

50

THE PADDOCKS

FI ELD

Hill Farm

Firs Farm

ROAD

GORDON ROAD

Lockhams Copse

3

Lower angfield Farm

CHAPEL

Curdridge

50

Wangfield Farm

Sch

The Vine School

Club

Titlarks Farm

CHURCH LANE

ST PETERS CL

Curdridge Common

LAKE ROAD

4

Cold Down Copse

VICARAGE

READING ROOM LA

LANE

BOTLEY LANE

The White House

Rec Grnd

Hall

WICKHAM

ROAD

LOCKHAMS LANE

KITNOCKS HILL

HILLSIDE

A334

50

Kitnocks House

Raglingto Farm

BOTLEY

STATION HILL

B3035

Kitnocks

Kitnocks Farm

Ferry Copse

5

LSONS RD

BOTLEY

A334

A3051

Woodview Park Caravan Site

Gibbets Corner

TEBOURBA WY LANE

OUTLANDS LANE

OUTLANDS LANE

Shawfords Lakes

nkmead Farm

Silford Copse

6

Trullmill Copse

Golf Course

Club House

ROAD Q

Fairthorne Grange

A3051

63

Hole Copse

E F G H

A   B   36   C   D

1

Park Lug

Woodmans Farm

Yewtree Farm

CURDRIDGE LANE

Works

CHASE GRO

CHASE LANE

GROV

THE POPLARS

BULL LANE

CLUB HOUSE LA

Rec Grnd

ASHLEY GDNS

LEAVES

Northcroft Farm

Nations Farm

Ash House

2

CURDRIDGE

Poplars Farmhouse

CURDRIDGE LANE

Curdridge Grange

SPENCER PLACE

Sandpits Copse

LITTLE BULL LA

BROOKLYNN

HOLE LANE

49

RDON ROAD

ms se

3

Long Acre Copse

SANDY

SANDY

Hilly Cantsley

Lyons Copse

Shedfield Grange

Meon Valley Golf & Country Club

Golf Course

ROAD

4

Wickham Vineyard

LANE

SANDY LANE

Shedfield House

Meon Valley

Shedfield

A334

49

Raglington Farm

Row Ash

Shedfield Lodge Nursing & Convalescent Home

ST ANNES LANE

ST JOHNS

Church Copse

CANFORD CL

SLOANE

PK

Cen Se

5

Ferry Copse

Hall Court

CHURCH

Shedfiel Common

Dugwells Farm

6

Hallcourt Wood

BIDDENFIELD

Brook Wood

LANE

Fordla Row

ole pse

A   B   C   D

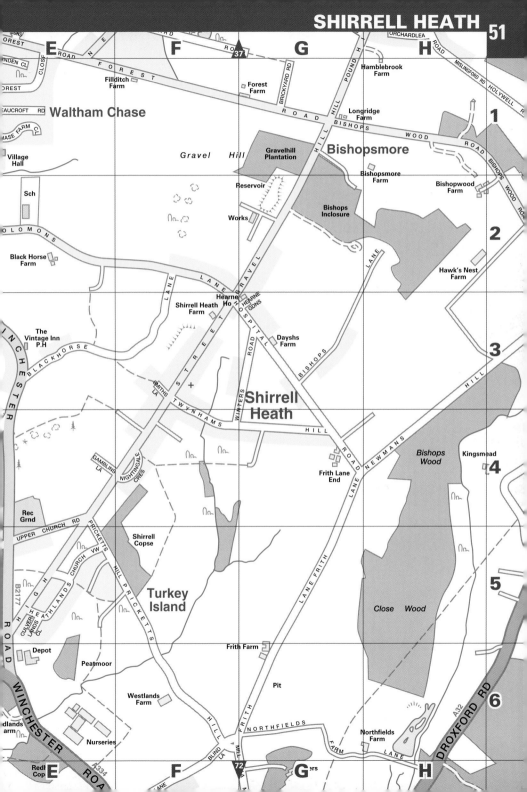

E   F   37   G   H

ORCHARDLEA

MISLINGFORD RD HOLYWELL R

Fildditch
Farm

FOREST ROAD

BRICKYARD RD

HILL POUND H

Hamblebrook
Farm

Forest
Farm

Longridge
Farm

BISHOPS   WOOD   ROAD   BISHOPS WOOD LANE

1

Waltham Chase

Village
Hall

Sch

Gravel   Hill

Gravelhill
Plantation

Reservoir

Works

Bishopsmore

Bishopsmore
Farm

Bishopwood
Farm

2

OLOMONS

Black Horse
Farm

LANE   LANE

Bishops
Inclosure

LANE

Hawk's Nest
Farm

Shirrell Heath
Farm

Hearne
Ho

HEARNE
GDNS

GRAVEL

HOSPITAL   ROAD

Dayshs
Farm

BISHOPS   HILL

3

WINCHESTER   ROAD

The
Vintage Inn
P.H

BLACKHORSE

SMITHS LA

STREET   TWYNHAMS

WINTERS

**Shirrell
Heath**

HILL

LANE NEWMANS

*Bishops
Wood*

Kingsmead

4

GAMBLINS LA

NIGHTINGALE CRES

Frith Lane
End

LANE FRITH

Rec
Grnd

UPPER   CHURCH   RD

PRICKETTS

CHURCH

VW

Shirrell
Copse

Shirrell Copse

5

B2177

HIGH

HEATHLANDS

CULVER
LANDS CL

HILL   PRICKETTS

**Turkey
Island**

Close   Wood

ROAD

Depot

Peatmoor

Westlands
Farm

Frith Farm

Pit

FRITH

DROXFORD RD

A32

6

WINCHESTER   ROAD   A334

dlands
arm

Nurseries

Northfields
Farm

LANE

Redh
Cop

E   F   72   G   H

HILL   BLIND LA   MILL   FRITH   NORTHFIELDS   FARM

A **B** **C** **D**

1

2

3

4

5

6

Biddlecombe Farm

The Marsh Farm

M27

38

ROMSEY ROAD

A31

WHITE HART LA

LYNDHURST ROAD

OLD

WITTENSFOR

C-WLAKE LA

CADNAM LA

CADNAM LA

OLD ROMSEY RD

SOUTHAMPTON

A31

A336

Cadnam

THE PARADE

Works

WELLINGTON

GREEN

FIR TREE RD

Barney Hay Farm

BARNEY HAYES

SOUTHAMPTON

Nursery

B3079

A31

M27 JUNCTION 1

A337

Rockram Wood

Home Farm

Bartley Lodge Hotel

LANE

ROAD

Cricket Ground

Beechwood

Park

Beechwood Farm

RO

Bart Mar

Shave Green Inclosure

Shave Hat

Shave Wood

Lambs Corner

BEECHWOOD

Beechwood House

Frenchs Bushes

P

P

ROAD

Yolsham Hill

Clay Hill

Nicholas Corner

BROCKISHILL

P

Hazel Hill

Brockis Hill

Brockishill Inclosure

Eave Hill

MINSTEAD

FOOTBALL GRN

Minstead Lodge

Brock Farm

Cricket Ground

ROAD

A337

A **B** **C** **D**

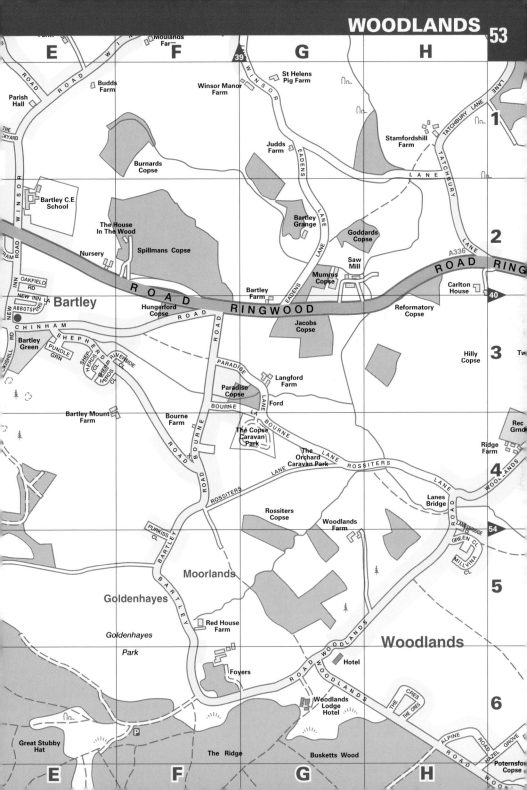

E HAM-BER WY DURLEY DENE WAY PENTRIDGE WY MILL WY IBBOTSON WY CHAPEL LA FAIRLEAD CL

RUSHINGTON BUSINESS PARK

NEW FOREST ENTERPRISE CENTRE

COCKLYDOWN WY ROCKLEIGH WY KENMORE WY FAIRMEAD

A326 BY-PASS

Cocklydown Copse

SPICERS HILL SPICERS ROAD LANE

PLAYERS CRES PLAYERS DRIVE

JACOBS WK JACOBS MOORCROSS

Office

F HOUNSDOWN ORCHARD CL MEADOW CL POWELL CRES AV PARKSIDE VALLEY ROAD BROOKS RIVERVIEW KIRK GDNS THE RETREAT

GUTTER Gutter

School

Newmans Copse

HOUNSDOWN BUSINESS PARK

NEWMANS COPSE RD

BULLS COPSE ROAD

Jacobs

41

G Bartley Water

MARCHWOOD

BY - PASS

GUTTER

Jacobs

Jacobs Farm

Bridge

P C **H** **C**

ELING HILL

BURY LANE

Cemy

Colbury Manor

ELING HILL

TROTT LANE

Eling Hill

Eling

Village Bells P.H

1

2

Hounsdown

Hall

HUNTERS HILL

A35

A35

LANE POUND

Colbury Farm

Bulls Copse

56

Trot

Trotts Farm

3

Hunters Inn Hill

Wildcolbury Wood

Pritchels Copse

Durley Farm

A326 M A

East Veugles Copse

Great Orchard Copse

Golts Copse

Fatroak Copse

Gregory Coopers Copse

4

Babley Row

OPEN FARM Longdown Dairy Farm

Muttonsnow Farm

Durleywild Copse

Knowles Copse

Great Cole Copse

Bowmoor Copse

Coffins Farm

56

Kites Copse

5

Blind Copse

Little Cole Copse

Pens Copse

Herons Hill

Great Herons Copse

Hall

Deerleap Farm

DEERLEAP

LANGLEY WOOD

Langley Lodge

Langley Pond

Withybeds Copse

Yards Hill

6

NATURE QUEST

DEERLEAP LANE

STAPLEW

Deerleap Inclosure

Parkers Cottages

E **F** The Homestead **G** **H** **S**

A   **B**   42   **C**   **D**

Channel

Hill

Eling

Village Bowls
P.H **1**

Works

Luggi Creek

Sewage
Works

Jubilee House
Customs & Exc

Goatee

Beach

Caravan
Site

PRINCE CHARLES
CONTAINER TERMINAL

RIVER

SOUTHAMPTON
DOCKS

TEST

MARCHWOOD

TROTTS

LANE

2

Bury
Copse

55

Trotts

Trotts
Farm

Bury
Farm

Bury Marsh

Slowhill
Copse

Jetty

QUAYSIDE

MARI

WALK

GMON
AM

Sewage
Works

Corks
Farm

Sparrows
Copse

BURY

ROAD

ROAD

NORMANDY

ADMIRALTY
MAGAZINE

3

East Veugles
Copse

A326

Spraggs
Copse

Bury Road

THE
GULLS

TIDES

SHORE

LANE

FIELD RD

TIDES

WAY

PEBBLE
CT

CORK

CT

OLD MAGAZINE CL

NORM

Tavells
Farm

MAIN

VALLEY
CL

THE
RUSHES

SHELL
CT

Coopers
pse **4**

MARCHWOOD

PARK

LANE

POOKS

Spraggs
Copse

Pooksgreen

BILBERRY DR

THE OWANS

ALDER CL

REED CL

TUSSOCKS

MOS

DR

MELICK

MARCHWOOD

AARON CL

POND

NORE

OLD CRAF

DRAKE

Coffins
Farm **55**

BOLHIN-
TOX AV

MARSHFIELD
CL

GREEN LONG

POPLAR DR

KESTREL CL

KINGFISHER

WOODPECKER

CRANBERRY

LICHEN WY

EVERGREEN CL

School

THE
HAWTHORNS

WOODGLADE CL

FERND

THO

KINGS

Kites
Copse **5**

STAPLEWOOD

LANE

THE CRES

LLOYD AV

OSPREY
CL

MOON

WOOD
SIDE CL

ST JOHNS
DR

SANDPIPER
CL

XCL

VILLAGE
CENTRE

VICARAGE

ROAD OAKLAND

HOUSE
GDNS

MALT

MAIN

NORMAN

CROOKED

DRIVE

Hill

Dumpers
Farm

Great Herons
Copse

Hammers
Copse

Parks
Farm

MAIN RD

THE

PLANTATION DR

LAKELAND
GDNS

VALE
WAY

AFRICA

MULBERRY

PHILPOTT

BURMA
WY

RD

SPINDLEWOOD

Pumpfie
Farm

Yards Hill **6**

Reeds Copse

Rudes
Copse

School

LARKSPUR

WILLOW
GDNS

DR

TWIGGS

BY - PASS

RO

Barrow Orchard
Copse

Stapleword
Cor **A**

LANE

TWIGGS

LANE

B Staplewood
Hill

A326

C

D he
ake

Grove Farm **E** **F** **G** **H**

NETLEY FIRS RD
NETLEY FIRS
FIRS DR
SAXON GDNS
GRAN CHURCH LA
JO
B3033
BURSLEDON ROAD
SMITH
YARDLEY RD
MORGAN
PARDOE
LINDEN
DUKE
HAVENDALE RD
CRUS

VICARAGE RD
PRETORIA RD
NORMAN
UPPER ST HELENS
NURSERY
ST HELENS ROAD
BRACKEN
PORTLET PL
COSTINA
FOXGLOVES
CLOSE AV
EDMUND
AMBLES

HALESDALE RD
GRANDA RD
TUDOR
ALEXANDRA RD
JUBILEE CT
CONISTON GDNS
ROSEMARY GNS
LOWER
GRO
TANHOUSE STOCK WOOD
FERNDALE AVE
TANHOUSE

WOODSIDE
ALBERT RD
DAMEN
Cemy
ROAD
HEATH HOUSE CL
NORRIS
Kings Copse County Primary School
PK CRAN-BOURNE
KINGS
TANHOUSE

1

E

KANES HILL
WOOD PK
N

WEST END ROAD

Netley Hill
NETLEY FIRS CL

Kanes Hill Caravan Site
BOTLEY RD

Sundays Hill
JOHNS ST

The Bonhomie Holiday Centre

PEEWIT HILL
PEEWIT HILL CL

WAYLANDS PL
FOORD ROAD
DOWNLAND RD
HEATH LANE
THE HAVEN

BOUNDARY ACRE

HUNTERS CT
DODWELL LANE

PYLANDS

Pilands Copse

HEATH HOUSE LANE
METU-CHEN WK
THURN TURMELL WK
BERGEN CRES
SHERWOOD AV
CRANBOURNE
PARK
Heath House Farm
TANHOUSE LANE
Hill

2

62

PEEWIT HILL
M27 JUNCTION 8
Bursledon Common

BERT BETTS WY
A3024

Dodwell Farm
PYLANDS LANE

Durncombs Copse
Sandpit Copse
Vantage Copse
Queen Elizabeth II Activities Centre
Hoe Moor Copse
Bottom Copse

3

A3024
WINDHOVER ROUNDABOUT
A27

Durncomb House
MANOR FARM COUNTRY PARK

4

Superstore
Bursledon Green
WINDMILL LANE
Windmill
Providence Hill

PROVIDENCE HILL
DEVONSHIRE GDNS
CAM-BRIAN
ASHLEY CRES
Phoenix
Lowford

BLUNDELL LANE
Bursledon Hall
OAKHILL

Catlan Copse

62
Boat Yard

5

SEAFORD CL
DILIGENCE WY
Comm Centre
PORTSMOUTH
LANCASTER
REDCROFT LA
RUTLAND GDNS
KINGSFIELD GDNS

OAKHILL TER
Oak Hill
DODWELL LANE
OAKHILL
BRIDGE

Brixedone Farm

RIVERVIEW TER

6

Claypits
Rec Grnd
Schools
Bursledon

THE GROVE
SPRING GRO
PINEVIEW CL
Rec Grnds
BURSLEDON HEIGHTS
OLD BRIDGE RD
HILL PLACE
JARVIS FIELDS

BLUNDELL LANE

Playing Field

Pilands Wood
Cemy
CHURCH LA

STATION RD
YACHTSMAN
SWAN
BURSLEDON
Rec Grnd
SWANWICK

BENTHAM
ANGLERS WY
WAYSIDE
COAL
S

ROMAN RD
SCHOOL RD
CHURCH LA
KEW
STREET
B3397
Swanwick Marina
ROAD
TOLLGATE
QUAY HAVEN
A27
SWANWICK BUSINESS CENTRE

65

E **F** **G** **H**

A   B   C   D

Pinkmead Copse

KINGS COPSE AV
PAXTON
ABRAHAM
PRECOSA
EDMUNDS RD
SALWAY
TILNEY
TICKELL
AMBLESIDE
KINGS CL
AV
RD

HAVENDALE RD
FERNDALE
TINHOUSE
CL COPSE
RO
S
AVENUE
HAVENDALE

Steeple Court

LANE
BROOK

CHUR
CHURCH LANE

1

Rec Grnd

Gould Copse

Manor Lodge

48

Manor Farm Museum

Marks Farm Chapel

C

Sew Wo

2

LANE TANHOUSE
LANE

Dockdell Copse LANE

Top

P

61

MANOR FARM COUNTRY PARK

Long Copse

3

Botto Copse

P

C

Fosters Copse

Dock Copse

HAMBLE

RIVER

Foxborrow Copse

Bloomfield Copse

Eyersdow Copse

4

Catland Copse

Swanwick Wood

Burridge Farm

Eyers Down Farm

BURRIDGE ROAD

61

Oaken Copse

Wellspring Copse

Burridge

Boat Yard

Lynwood

GREEN LANE

5

RO

Air Traffic Control Centre

NATURE RESERVE

ROAD

Sweet Farm

Playing Field

RIVERVIEW
TER
PARK

OLDEN

Brickworks Museum

LAWSON
COAL
SOPWITH

NEW LANE

Nurseries

BOTLEY

A3051

ANDALUSIAN
SWEET
GDNS
CAMARGUE CRES
LIPIZZANER FLDS

6

Lower Swanwick

EMSBANK
RD
BENTHAM WY
WAYSIDE
ANGLERS WY
QUAY
IBIL
LOWER
SWANWICK RD

M27

WANWICK

LANE

WALPOLE

GLEN RD

Glen House

Swanwick

The Elm Tree P.H

BOTLEY RD

ASHLEY
YEW
SUFFOLK
HILLS

SWANWICK BUSINESS CENTRE

A   B   C   D

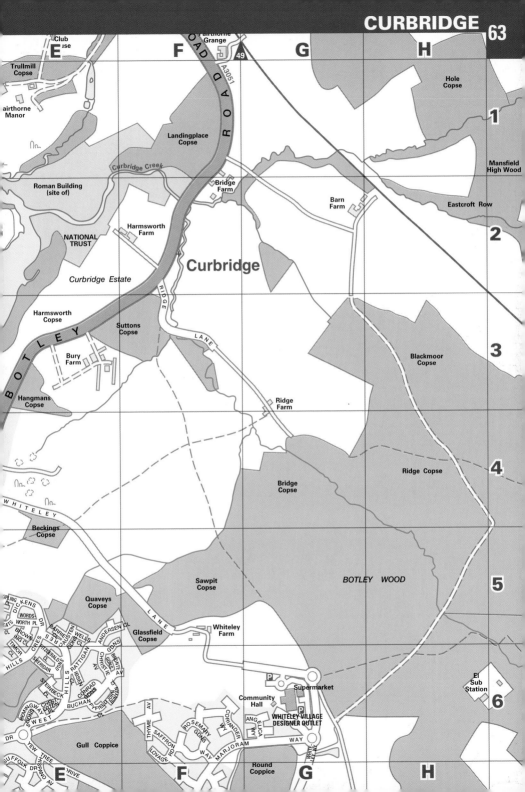

E · F · G · H

1 · 2 · 3 · 4 · 5 · 6

Club
ise

Trullmill
Copse

airthorne
Manor

Fairthorne
Grange

A3051

ROAD

Hole
Copse

Mansfield
High Wood

Landingplace
Copse

Curbridge Creek

Roman Building
(site of)

Bridge
Farm

Barn
Farm

Eastcroft Row

Harmsworth
Farm

NATIONAL
TRUST

Curbridge

Curbridge Estate

RIDGE

Harmsworth
Copse

Suttons
Copse

LANE

Blackmoor
Copse

BOTLEY

Bury
Farm

Hangmans
Copse

Ridge
Farm

Ridge Copse

WHITELEY

Bridge
Copse

Beckings
Copse

LANE

Sawpit
Copse

BOTLEY WOOD

Quaveys
Copse

Glassfield
Copse

Whiteley
Farm

El
Sub
Station

KIPLING DR · DICKENS CL · KEATS CL · WORDSWORTH PL · BROWNING CL · BARRIE CRES · WELLS RD · CALDIST RD · ANDERSEN CL · GDNS · BRONTE GDNS · CHRISTIE AV

STEINBECK CL · SHERIDAN CL · STRATHEARN RATTIGAN AV · IBSEN · CONRAD GDNS · TWYFORD · BUCHAN · CHEKOV CL · SWEET

HILLS · HEMINGWAY · GOLDING CL · SUFFOLK DR · YEW TREE DRIVE · THORNO AV

Gull Coppice

THYME AV · SAFFRON RD · LOVAGE · ROSEMARY GDNS · CORIANDER WY · MARJORAM WAY · ANGELICA WAY · WHITE LEVEE

Community
Hall

Supermarket

**WHITELEY VILLAGE
DESIGNER OUTLET**

Round
Coppice

WAY

Swanwick Marina

E B3397 F ACORNS KEW G H

MALLARDS ROAD HUNGERFORD KEW LANE CHURCH LA STREET LANDS END ROAD

1

Stones HIGH SALTERNS LA Hacketts Marsh

Mallards Moor SALTERNS LANE Lincegrove Marsh

2

Hound Farm Sewage Works Pontoons

Hound ROAD Tip (disused) Badnam Copse Badnam Creek

Academy Hound Manor SATCHELL Badnam Copse Boat Yard

3

HAMBLE BROADWAY Playing Field School Mercury Yacht Marina

HAMBLE Riverside Caravan Site Downkiln Copse

Playing Field THE HARDS FISHER KING HAMBLE

Hospital Cemetery Sports Ground FRY CL MATHAS MARINERS CL

Works AIRFIELD (Disused) LAST AG RD MERCURY GDNS CERDIC MWS Satchell Marsh Pier

4

School THE CLOSE SATCHELL

Mount Pleasant Recreation Ground RIVER

Sports Ground LANE Works OAKWOOD WY Port Hamble Marina Bunny Meadows

5

KINGS AV VERDON TUTOR SYDNEY AV CLOSE GARDENS CROWSPORT ESTATE

WAY HAMBLE SYDNEY CRES AV ASTRAL CL BARTON DR BARTON DR SPITFIRE WY SPITFIRE WY Hamble Marina Dr SATCHELL LANE R.A.F. Yacht Club

CHALMERS WY NORBURY GDNS GRANTHAM AV FLOWERS CL BEAULIEU RD DEANFIELD RD PEGASUS COLLEGE CL SPITFIRE CIRRUS GDNS ANTARES BLDGS HAMBLE HOUSE LA Hamble House WELL THE HIGH Royal Southern Yacht Club

6

BEECH GDNS SOUTHO WESTFIELD CLOSE COACH BEECH CL WAY LANE HIGH HALL Club Works Fire Sta HAMBLE SIDE COPSE STREET B3397 RIVER GRN THE SQ HAMBLE MANOR P P

COMMON BEECH CL ENSIGN SIGN MITCHELL PK LANE **Hamble-le-Rice** SCHOOL LANE SOLENT MDWS Hamble Green P

Solent Way BP Oil Storage Depot EMMONS VAN LA OLD PRIORY CL ADMIRALS CT LANE Admirals Green

E F 72 G Ferry H

A   B   C   D

1

Church Farm
Lych Gate
Bramshot Hill
Locks Farm
Dibden Manor Hotel
HILL MAIN
Dibden
LOCKS COTTAGES
BY-PASS HYTHE
A326
GARDEN CITY
BRAMSHOTT ROAD
The Old Manor
MANOR RD

2

Dale Farm
MANOR ROAD
Club House
Dibden Golf Course
Applemore Hill
Roys Copse
WAY
CLAYPITS
Talbot Farm
ROAD
LANE
SOUTHAMPTON R
Home Farm
Clayfield Sports Centre

Applemore

3

hwood osure
Sleepy Hollow
Holly Lodge Farm
Riding School
BY-PASS HYTHE
SIZER WAY
RANMORE CT
Drapers Copse Caravan Site
CHALLENGER WAY
Drapers Copse
Fern Hill
TAMAR
CORSAIR DR
CAVALIER CHEVO

4

Superstore
SIZER WAY
CLAYPITS LA
CYGNUS GDNS
Applemore Sports Centre
Tumulus
Schools
REDWOOD CL
BEECHWOOD
ALDERWOOD CL
CUMBERLAND
CANTERBURY
CABOT DR
CHARIOT DR
CAMBRIA DR
CALEDONIA
CORDELIA
CORINNA GDNS
CHALLENGER WAY
CORNWALLIS
PENNINE WY
MENDIP
BRECON
MALVERN
School
Playing Field
School

5

den Bottom
Horestone Hill
ROMAN BY-PASS
Dibden Purlieu
NASH ROAD
ROMAN WY
WELLINGTON CT
OAKLANDS
BRINKSWOOD
HUXLEYWOOD
MILNE CL
BEECHWOOD
BUCKMAN CT
DOWN WOOD
LIME CT
NORTH
WATER
WALK
WEST
OAK CL
HAYNES
NOADS

6

The Noads
A326
B3054
HYTHE M
BEAULIEU
LINEDALE
ROMAN ROAD
OAK ROAD
TALBOT RD
MANSELL
Sch
P
Dibden Inclosure

A   B   C   D

E
F
G
H
1
2
3
4
5
6
RIVER TEST
Lock
Slipway
Ferry Landing Stage
Hythe Pier
Hythe Hard
Pier Railway
HYTHE MARINA
WHITE HEATHER CT
VELSHEDA CT
VELSHEDA CT
ASTRA CT
ENDEAVOUR WY
SHAMROCK WY
West Cliff Hall
JESSOP WK
WATERSIDE
MOUNT HOUSE CL
Pol Sta
Recreation Ground
PROSPECT PL
Hythe
THE PROMENADE
HIGH ST
THE MARSH
ST JOHNS ST
Comm Centre
School
Library
Fire Sta
DIBDEN LODGE CL
SOUTHAMPTON ROAD
JONES LANE
WEST BEAUMARIS GDNS
MOUNTFIELD
MULLINS LANE
MICHAELS WY
DOUGLAS WY
ROBERTS RD
SOLENT DR
HOLLYBANK RD
FAIRWAY RD
LOWER MULLINS LA
DALE RD
MERRIVALE
LAUREL CL
CONIFER CL
SYCAMORE RD
COPSEWOOD RD
HILLVIEW
FERN RD
LANEHAYS RD
FERRY RD
HOLLYBANK CL
GREEN CL
CRESCENT RD
SCHOOL RD
ALEXANDRA RD
EDWARD RD
LONGMEADOW GDNS
ATHELING RD
SOUTH STREET
SPRING RD
MOUSEHOLE LA
COAT GDNS
RACKETTS
KELVIN
FAIRVIEW DR
WHITTINGTON CL
FAIRVIEW CL
LANGDOWN FIRS
Rec Grnd
LANGDOWN LAWN
WINDRUSH WY
HOBART DR
LANGDOWN RD
ASHFORD CRES
HIRST RD
SEWARD RD
GRAYS AV
Sch
DRIVE
HARVEY GDNS
SHORE ROAD
SCOTT-PAINE DR
WADMORE CL
DAVIDSON CL
SELMAN CL
EMERALD CRES
SIR CHRISTOPHER CT
DOMINY CL
Slipway
Pontoons
Pier
Hythe Sailing Club
Hall
Nature Reserve
Shore Road Playing Field
Langdown
Tates Copse
TATES RD
HOME FARM CL
Sewage Works
Pipers Copse
GUILLEMOT CL
GANNET CL
CORMORANT DR
FULMAR DRIVE
CURLEW DR
CURLEW WK
TERN CL
FROST LANE
HART HILL
Furzey Holts
Furzey Piece
Buttash Wood
PINEWOOD CRES
SPINNEY DALE
Hotel
Frostlane Copse
Furzedown Farm
Frostlane
Kitchers Copse
Crampool Copse
Gringos Copse
Seadown Veterinary Hospital
Forest Lodge
Forest Lodge Farm
Buttsash
HYTHE & DIBDEN HOSPITAL
HIGHLANDS WY
BELVEDERE RD
DUKESWOOD DR
WHITEWATER RISE
BEAULIEU RD
GOLDEN HIND PK
ARMADA DR
DEERLEAP WAY
ELGIN CL
QUEENS CL
KNIGHTWOOD RD
BURNETT CL
LYTTON RD
FURZEY AVENUE
LADYCROSS RD
FOXBURY CL
ROSEBERY AV
LINWOOD CL
BRIDGE
BUTTS
GREATWOOD CL
FROGHALL
SADLERS
ELIZABETH GDNS
CHALONER CRES
ASH
AVENUE
PARTRIDGE RD
BULLRUSH CL
Schs
CRETE LA
HEATHERSTONE AV
BEVERLEY RD
MONKS WK
ARNWOOD AV
HAYLEY CL
BUTTS ASH GDNS
BLENHEIM MWS
YELVERTON AV
FLEURET CL
ASHLEIGH CL
FAWLEY ROAD
CRESCENT
BEECH CL
FOREST MDW
FOREST FRONT
CHARLESTON RD
EAST
Work
Wor
PASS

E F G H

64

1

2

3

4

5

6

Pipe Line

Outfall

Pipe Line

Works

ROAD

ROAD

EAST

HARLESTON

ROAD

Great Stiles Wood

Works

Wks

CADLAND

Lammas Wood

Mud & Sand

Cadland Creek

Reservoir

Flare Stack

Street

Street

Sewage Works

FOURTEENTH

THIRTEENTH

Street

TWELFTH ST

TWELFTH

ELEVENTH ST

ELEVENTH

AVENUE

AVENUE

STREET

STREET

AVENUE

D

E

F

STREET

SEVENTH ST

SIXTH ST

SIXTH AV

FIFTH ST

FIFTH

SEVENTH ST

AVENUE

OIL   REFINERY

AVENUE

STREET

STREET

AVENUE

STREET

C

Pipe Line

AVENUE

AVENUE

AVENUE

Holbury

ROVE LONG AV

STEPHEN

SPRINGFIELD

SPRINGFIELD

STANLEY

ALTONS

CT

RD

SLOANE

CP

A426

LANE

GRO

LANE

A

TENTH

NINTH AVENUE

EIGHTH AVENUE

SEVENTH ST

AVENUE

B

Flare Stack

FIFTH

SIXTH ST

SEVENTH ST

AVENUE

STREET

FOURTH AV

Flare Stack

AVENUE

STREET

THIRD AV

AVENUE

STREET SECOND

AVENUE

FIRST

STREET

C

MARSH LANE

MARSH LA

CHI

70

71

E F G H

REFINERY

E · F · G · H

69

THIRD ST · SECOND · AVENUE · STREET · FIRST STREET · CHURCH LA MARSH LA · CHURCH · A AVENUE · CHURCH CL · CHURCH LANE · ORCHARD LA · FOREST EDGE · WOODVILLE RD · COLEVILLE RD · LINDA RD · THE A? · PADDOCKS · MEAD · SCHOOL RD CHOOL · FALCON FIELDS · FENN · CHARLES · LEY CL · SHERRY · COPTHORNE CL · COPTHORNE · CL · COPTHORNE · Libby's Hall · THE FORGE · THE SO · ROAD · THE · LANE · WHITE'S · ASHLETT CL · ASHLETT · HALL MWS · RYME · HALSTOT RD · Quay · ROAD · STONEHILLS

Fawley

ASHDOWN · ASHDOWN RD · SLADES HILL · THE PENTAG · BLACKFIELD RD · CHAPEL LA · ROAD · FAWLEY · B3053

FAWLEY BY-PASS

The Pentagon

DUN FIELD COPSE · DEVY · ROAD · TOOMER CL · DBEVIS · ROAD SMITH · THORNHILL CL · LIGHT · THORNHILL RD · FOUR · SHS BELL · MILLIKEN · KING · RDS · JONES · CL · CLES · FEATHER · FUREY · HEDLEY

FAWLEY BY-PASS · B3053

Fields Farm

Fields Heath

COPSE · COPSE · LANE · DS · SAXON · DYKE · WESSEX CT · CEDRIC · ROAD · VIKING CL · SOUTH GREEN LANE

Toms Down

Queen Elizabeth II Recreation Ground

Mopley Pond

Tom's Down

Badminston Common

BADMINSTON LANE

Badminston Plantation

Sprat's Down

WALKERS LANE · AV · LANE · POLE · Y

CLARE · GDNS · FOX · GDNS · LA · FOXS WYES · FORESTGATE · LA GLADE

Dean's Bridge

Spratsdown Plantation

Newhouse Copse

FORGE · ROAD · LEPE · ROAD

Kings Rew Copse

Stanswood Common

Whitefield Farm · orthwork

STANSWOOD ROAD

E · F · G · H

1 · 2 · 3 · 4 · 5 · 6

A - Z INDEX TO STREETS
with Postcodes

The Index includes some names for which there is insufficient space on the maps. These names are indicated by an * and are followed by the nearest adjoining thoroughfare.

A Avenue SO45   68 D5
Aaron Ct SO40   56 D4
Abbey Cl SO45   67 F3
Abbey Hill SO31   64 A1
Abbey Pk Ind Est
SO51   18 B2
Abbey Water SO51   17 E1
Abbeyfields Cl SO31   64 D2
Abbots Way SO31   64 D2
Abbotsbury Rd SO50   22 D5
Abbotsfield Cl SO16   29 G5
Abbotsford SO40   53 E3
Abbotswood Cl SO51   10 A4
Abbotts Rd SO50   31 G1
Abbotts Way SO17   44 C2
Abbottsfield SO40   41 E4
Abercrombie Gdns
SO16   29 E6
Aberdeen Rd SO17   45 E3
Aberdour Cl SO18   45 H3
Abingdon Gdns SO16   29 H6
Above Bar St SO14   4 D1
Abraham Cl SO30   48 A6
Acacia Rd SO19   59 G1
Acorn Cl SO40   57 E5
Acorn Cl SO31   65 E5
Acorn Dr SO16   28 C3
Acorn Gro SO53   20 A3
Adams Cl SO30   47 G1
Adams Rd SO45   67 F4
Adams Wood Dr SO40   56 D5
Adamson Cl SO53   13 E5
Adcock Ct SO16   28 C3
Addis Sq SO17   44 C3
Addison Cl SO51   9 H4
Addison Rd SO50   21 H2
Adela Verne Cl SO19   60 C3
Adelaide Rd SO17   44 C3
Adey Cl SO19   60 A4
Admirals Cl SO45   71 G1
Admirals Ct SO31   72 C1
Admirals Way SO40   67 G2
Admiralty Way SO40   56 D3
Adur Cl SO18   46 A3
Africa Dr SO40   56 C5
Aikman La SO40   40 C4
Ailsa La SO19   59 E2
Ainsley Gdns SO50   21 H3
Aintree Cl SO50   33 H3
Aintree Rd SO40   40 D2
Alan Drayton Way
SO50   22 D6
Alandale Rd SO19   60 B2
Albany Ct SO32   36 A1
Albany Dr SO32   36 A1
Albany Rd,
Bishops Waltham
SO32   36 A2
Albany Rd,
Holbury SO45   68 D6
Albany Rd,
Romsey SO51   9 F6
Albany Rd,
Southampton SO15   43 G5
Albert Cl SO31   64 C3
Albert Rd,
Bishops Waltham
SO32   36 B2
Albert Rd,
Eastleigh SO50   22 A3
Albert Rd,
Hedge End SO30   61 F1
Albert Rd North SO14   5 G5
Albert Rd South SO14   5 G5
Albion Pl SO14   4 D4
Albury Pl SO53   12 C5
Alcantara Cres SO14   5 G5
Alder Cl,
Dibden Purlieu SO45   66 C4
Alder Cl,
Marchwood SO40   56 C4
Alder Cl, Romsey SO51   18 B1
Alder Cl,
Winchester SO21   15 E5
Alder Hill Dr SO40   40 C4
Alder Rd SO16   28 D6
Aldermoor Av SO16   29 E6
Aldermoor Cl SO16   29 D6
Aldermoor Rd SO16   28 D6
Alderney Cl SO16   28 C6
Alderwood Av SO53   20 C2
Alexander Cl SO40   40 D4

Alexandra Cl SO45   67 F3
Alexandra Rd,
Eastleigh SO53   13 G6
Alexandra Rd,
Hedge End SO30   61 F1
Alexandra Rd,
Hythe SO45   67 F2
Alexandra Rd,
Southampton SO15   4 A1
Alexandra Way SO30   48 C5
Alfred Cl SO40   40 C4
Alfred Rose Ct SO18   31 F6
Alfred St SO14   44 C6
Alfriston Gdns SO19   60 A2
Allan Gro SO51   9 H6
Allbrook Hill SO50   22 A1
Allbrook Knoll SO50   21 H1
Allbrook Way SO50   13 H5
Allen Rd SO30   47 G5
Allerton Cl SO40   40 D3
Allington La,
Eastleigh SO50   33 E4
Allington La,
Southampton SO30   32 A6
Allington Rd SO15   42 B4
Allotment Rd*,
St Johns Rd SO30   61 E2
Alma La SO32   24 D6
Alma Rd, Romsey SO51   9 F6
Alma Rd,
Southampton SO14   44 B4
Almatade Rd SO18   45 H5
Almond Rd SO15   43 G6
Alpine Cl SO18   46 A3
Alpine Rd SO40   53 H6
Alton Cl SO50   23 G5
Alum Cl SO45   70 C1
Alum Way SO18   46 A5
Amberley Cl,
Botley SO30   48 C4
Amberley Cl,
North Baddesley SO52   18 C3
Amberley Ct SO40   41 E6
Amberslade Walk SO45   67 E5
Amberwood Cl SO40   40 C2
Ambleside,
Bishops Waltham
SO32   36 A2
Ambleside,
Botley SO30   62 A1
Ambleside Gdns SO19   59 H3
Amey Gdns SO40   40 B2
Amoy St SO15   44 A6
Ampthill Rd SO15   43 F5
Ancasta Rd SO14   44 C5
Andalusian Gdns PO15   62 D6
Anderby Rd SO16   42 B2
Andersen Cl PO15   63 E5
Anderson Cl SO51   10 A4
Andersons Rd SO14   5 G5
Andes Cl SO14   5 G5
Andes Rd SO16   41 H1
Andover Rd SO15   4 A1
Andrew Cl,
Dibden Purlieu SO45   67 F6
Andrew Cl,Totton SO40   40 D5
Andrewes Cl SO21   36 C1
Anfield Cl SO50   33 G1
Angel Cres SO18   45 H5
Angelica Gdns SO50   33 G3
Angelica Way PO15   63 G6
Anglers Way SO31   61 H6
Anglesea Cl SO15   43 F3
Anglesea Rd SO15   43 F3
Anglesea Ter SO14   5 G4
Anson Dr SO19   60 B1
Anson Rd SO50   33 H2
Anstey Rd SO51   9 H4
Anton Cl SO51   10 A6
Anvil Cl SO30   48 B2
Apollo Pl SO18   45 H4
Appleton Rd SO18   45 F3
Appletree Cl SO40   40 C3
Appletree Ct SO30   48 C5
Applewood Gdns
SO19   59 H3
Applewood Pl SO40   40 C6
April Cl SO18   46 A5
Apsley Pl SO53   12 C5
Aquila Way SO31   65 F6
Arcadia Cl SO16   43 F1
Archers Cl SO40   40 D2
Archers Rd,
Eastleigh SO50   21 H4
Archers Rd,
Southampton SO15   44 A5
Archery Gdns SO19   59 G4
Archery Gro SO19   59 F4

Archery Rd SO19   59 F4
Archway St SO16   31 E5
Arden Cl SO18   46 A3
Ardingly Cres SO30   48 A2
Ardnave Cres SO16   30 A4
Argyle Rd SO14   5 E1
Arliss Rd SO16   43 E2
Arlott Ct SO15   44 A4
Armada Cl SO16   28 C3
Armada Dr SO45   67 E4
Armitage Av SO45   67 E6
Armstrong Ct SO16   28 D4
Arnheim Cl SO16   29 G6
Arnheim Rd SO16   29 G6
Arnold Rd,
Eastleigh SO50   31 H1
Arnold Rd,
Southampton SO17   44 D2
Arnwood Av SO45   68 A2
Arreton SO31   64 C1
Arrow Cl,
Eastleigh SO50   21 H3
Arrow Cl,
Southampton SO19   59 E5
Arthur Rd,
Eastleigh SO50   21 H3
Arthur Rd,
Southampton SO15   43 H5
Arthurs Gdns SO30   47 G1
Arun Rd SO18   46 A1
Arundel Rd,
Eastleigh SO50   21 H2
Arundel Rd,
Southampton SO40   41 G4
Ascot Rd SO30   33 H2
Ascupart St SO14   5 F3
Asford Gro SO50   22 B4
Ash Cl,
Bursledon SO31   61 E6
Ash Cl, Hythe SO45   68 B2
Ash Cl,
North Baddesley SO52   18 D3
Ash Cl,
Thornhill Park SO19   46 B6
Ash Cl, Whitenap SO51   18 A1
Ash Cl,
Winchester SO21   15 E5
Ash Gro SO40   54 C3
Ash Rd SO40   54 B4
Ash Tree Rd SO18   45 F3
Ashbridge Rise SO53   12 C5
Ashburnham Cl SO19   59 F1
Ashburton Cl SO45   66 C3
Ashby Cres SO40   40 D5
Ashby Rd,
Southampton SO19   60 A3
Ashby Rd,Totton SO40   40 D5
Ashdene SO15   43 E4
Ashdene Rd SO40   54 C4
Ashdown Cl SO53   12 D3
Ashdown Dr SO53   12 D3
Ashdown Rd,
Eastleigh SO53   12 D4
Ashdown Rd,
Southampton SO45   71 E2
Ashdown Way SO51   9 H6
Ashen Cl SO53   13 E5
Ashford Cres SO45   67 G3
Ashlea Cl SO50   23 H6
Ashleigh Cl SO45   68 B2
Ashlett Cl SO45   71 G1
Ashlett Mews SO45   71 G1
Ashlett Rd SO45   71 G1
Ashley Cl SO31   62 D6
Ashley Cres SO19   60 B4
Ashley Cross Cl SO45   70 B1
Ashley Ct SO31   61 F4
Ashley Gdns,
Eastleigh SO53   21 F3
Ashley Gdns,
Southampton SO31   50 D1
Ashley Mdws SO51   9 G5
Ashmead Rd SO16   42 D1
Ashridge Cl SO15   44 A4
Ashton Cl SO32   35 H1
Ashton La SO32   35 H1
Ashton Pl SO53   12 C4
Ashtree Ct*,
Chestnut Cl SO40   20 D5
Ashurst Bridge Rd
SO40   40 C6
Ashurst Cl,
Ashurst SO40   54 C4
Ashurst Cl,
Southampton SO19   59 H5
Ashwood Gdns,
Southampton SO16   43 H1
Ashwood Gdns,
Totton SO40   40 D5

Aspen Cl,
Southampton SO30   48 A5
Aspen Cl,
Winchester SO21   15 F5
Aspen Holt SO16   30 B4
Aspen Walk SO40   40 C4
Aster Rd SO16   30 D6
Astra Ct SO45   67 F1
Astral Gdns SO31   65 F5
Asturias Way SO14   5 G5
Asylum Rd SO15   4 D1
Atheling Rd SO45   67 F3
Athelstan Rd SO19   45 F5
Athena Cl SO50   23 F5
Atherfield Rd SO16   42 B1
Atherley Ct SO15   43 H4
Atherley Rd SO15   43 H5
Atlantic Cl SO14   58 D4
Atlantic Park Vw SO18   45 H1
Attwoods Dro SO21   6 B3
Auckland Rd SO15   42 C5
Audley Pl SO50   23 E6
Augustine Rd SO14   5 G1
Augustus Cl SO53   13 G6
Augustus Way SO53   13 F6
Austen Cl SO40   41 E5
Austen Gdns PO15   63 E5
Autumn Pl SO17   44 B4
Autumn Rd SO40   57 E5
Avebury Gdns SO50   12 C4
Avenger Cl SO53   20 D2
Avens Cl SO50   33 H3
Avenue Rd SO14   44 B4
Avington Cl SO50   22 C3
Avington Ct SO16   30 A6
Avon Cres SO51   10 A6
Avon Ct SO31   64 C3
Avon Grn SO53   21 E2
Avon Rd SO18   45 G3
Avonborne Way SO53   12 C6
Avro Cl SO15   42 D5

B Avenue SO45   69 E5
Back of the Walls SO14   4 D6
Bacon Cl SO19   59 G5
Baddesley Cl SO52   18 D2
Baddesley Rd SO52   12 B5
Baden Powell Way
SO51   9 F6
Bader Cl SO30   47 G4
Badger Cl SO50   23 E6
Badger Ct SO50   23 E6
Badger Farm Rd SO23   6 C1
Badgers Walk SO45   67 F5
Badminston La SO45   71 G3
Bagber Rd SO40   41 F5
Bagshot Mews SO19   59 G3
Bailey Cl SO30   48 C5
Bailey Grn SO18   45 H2
Bakers Dro SO16   28 C5
Balaclava Rd SO18   45 H4
Balfour Rd SO19   60 A1
Ballard Cl SO16   42 A3
Balmoral Cl,
Eastleigh SO53   12 C5
Balmoral Cl,
Southampton SO16   29 G4
Balmoral Way SO16   28 B4
Baltic Rd SO30   46 D2
Bampton Ct SO53   20 D2
Banbury Av SO19   60 B1
Bangor Rd SO15   43 F5
Banister Cl SO15   44 A5
Banister Mews SO15   44 A5
Banister Rd SO15   44 A5
Bank St SO32   36 C2
Bankside SO18   31 F6
Banning St SO51   17 E1
Barbe Baker Av SO30   46 B2
Barberry Dr SO40   40 B3
Barclay Mews SO45   68 B2
Barford Cl SO53   12 C6
Bargate Centre
SO14   4 D4
Bargate St SO14   4 D4
Barker Mill Cl SO16   28 C3
Barle Cl SO18   46 A1
Barleycorn Walk SO40   52 C1
Barn Piece SO53   20 B1
Barnes Cl SO18   46 B5
Barnes Rd SO19   46 B6
Barney Hayes La SO40   52 D2
Barnfield Cl SO19   59 F5
Barnfield Ct SO19   59 F5
Barnfield Way SO19   59 G5
Barnsfield Cres SO40   40 A5
Barnsland SO30   46 A1
Baron Rd SO31   65 F5

Barons Mead SO16   42 C1
Barrie Cl PO15   63 E5
Barrington Cl SO50   21 G2
Barrow Down Gdns
SO19   60 D2
Barrow Hill Rd SO40   39 F4
Barry Rd SO19   46 A6
Barters Cl SO16   42 D3
Bartley Av SO40   41 E6
Bartley Rd SO40   53 F5
Barton Cl SO51   9 H5
Barton Cres SO18   45 G3
Barton Dr,
Hamble SO31   65 F5
Barton Dr,
Hedge End SO30   47 H5
Barton Pk Ind Est
SO50   22 A5
Barton Rd SO50   22 A5
Bartram Rd SO40   41 G6
Barwell Ter SO30   48 A6
Basing Mews*,
Basingwell St SO32   36 C2
Basing Way SO53   20 C4
Basingwell St SO32   36 C2
Bassett Av SO16   30 B5
Bassett Cl SO16   30 B6
Bassett Cres East
SO16   30 B6
Bassett Cres West
SO16   30 A6
Bassett Ct SO16   30 A6
Bassett Dale SO16   30 A4
Bassett Gdns SO16   30 A6
Bassett Green Cl SO16   30 C4
Bassett Green Ct SO16   30 D5
Bassett Green Dr SO16   30 B4
Bassett Green Rd SO16   30 B3
Bassett Green Village
SO16   30 C5
Bassett Heath Av SO16   30 A3
Bassett Mdw SO16   30 A6
Bassett Mews SO16   30 A5
Bassett Row SO16   30 A4
Bassett Wood Dr SO16   30 B4
Bassett Wood Rd SO16   30 B4
Batchelor Grn SO31   61 E5
Bath Cl SO19   46 A6
Bath Rd SO19   46 A6
Bath St SO14   44 B5
Battery Hill SO32   36 A2
Baxter Rd SO19   60 D1
Bay Cl SO19   59 H3
Bay Rd SO19   59 H3
Bay Tree Gdns SO40   56 D4
Bay Trees SO19   46 D6
Beach La SO31   64 A2
Beacon Cl SO16   28 B3
Beacon Mews SO30   46 C4
Beacon Rd SO30   46 C3
Bealing Cl SO16   30 D6
Bearslane Cl SO40   40 D3
Beatrice Rd SO15   43 G5
Beattie Rise SO30   47 H2
Beatty Ct SO19   60 B1
Beaucroft Rd SO32   51 E1
Beaufort Dr SO32   36 B2
Beaulieu Cl SO16   29 F5
Beaulieu Rd,
Dibden Purlieu SO45   66 D6
Beaulieu Rd,
Eastleigh SO50   21 H4
Beaulieu Rd,
Hamble SO31   65 E5
Beaumaris Cl SO53   20 B4
Beaumaris Gdns SO45   67 E2
Beaumont Cl SO16   30 A6
Beaumont Rd SO40   41 G4
Beauworth Av SO18   46 B3
Beaver Dr SO50   23 E6
Bedford Av SO19   59 F4
Bedford Cl SO30   48 A6
Bedford Pl SO15   4 D1
Bedwell Cl SO16   28 D4
Beech Av SO18   45 F5
Beech Cl,
Eastleigh SO53   13 E5
Beech Cl,
Romsey SO51   18 A2
Beech Cl,
Southampton SO31   65 E6
Beech Copse SO16   42 D3
Beech Cres SO45   68 B2
Beech Gdns SO31   65 E6
Beech Rd,
Ashurst SO40   54 C4
Beech Rd,
Eastleigh SO53   13 E5
Beech Rd,
Hedge End SO30   47 H5

Beech Rd,
Southampton SO15 43 F6
Beechcroft Cl SO53 21 E2
Beechcroft Way SO53 21 F2
Beechdale Cl SO40 40 D2
Beechdale Walk SO40 40 D2
Beeches Hill SO32 36 C1
Beechfield Ct SO15 33 E4
Beechmount Rd SO16 30 B5
Beechwood Cl SO53 12 C4
Beechwood Cres SO53 12 C4
Beechwood Gdns
SO18 45 G4
Beechwood Rd,
Bartley SO40 52 C4
Beechwood Rd,
Holbury SO45 70 B1
Beechwood Rise SO18 46 B3
Beechwood Way SO45 66 C4
Begonia Rd SO16 30 C6
Belbins SO51 9 F1
Belgrave Ind Est
SO17 44 D1
Belgrave Rd SO17 44 D2
Bell Cl SO45 71 E3
Bell St, Romsey SO51 17 E1
Bell St,
Southampton SO14 5 E4
Bellamy Ct SO17 45 E3
Bellemoor Rd SO15 43 G3
Bellevue Rd,
Eastleigh SO50 21 H4
Bellevue Rd,
Southampton SO15 44 B6
Bellvue Ter SO14 44 B6
Bellflower Way SO53 12 B6
Belmont Cl SO45 67 F5
Belmont Rd,
Eastleigh SO53 21 F2
Belmont Rd,
Southampton SO17 44 D4
Belstone Rd SO40 41 F5
Belton Rd SO19 60 A3
Belvedere Rd SO45 67 F5
Belvidere Rd SO14 5 G2
Belvidere Ter SO14 5 G1
Bembridge SO31 64 C2
Bembridge Cl SO16 30 D4
Benbow Gdns SO40 40 D2
Benedict Cl SO51 18 A1
Benhams Farm Cl
SO18 45 H3
Benhams Rd SO18 45 H3
Benmore Gdns SO53 12 C6
Benny Hill Cl SO50 21 G5
Benson Rd SO15 43 F4
Bentham Ct SO16 30 B6
Bentham Way SO31 61 H6
Bentley Grn SO18 46 B4
Bere Cl SO53 12 B6
Beresford Cl SO53 21 F2
Beresford Gdns SO53 21 F2
Beresford Rd SO53 21 F2
Bergen Cres SO30 61 G1
Berkeley Cl SO15 44 A5
Berkeley Gdns SO15 61 G1
Berkeley Rd SO15 44 A5
Bernard St SO14 4 D5
Bernwood Gro SO45 70 D5
Berry Cl SO19 47 H6
Berry La SO21 7 E5
Berrywood Bsns Village
SO30 47 F1
Berrywood Gdns SO30 47 F4
Bert Betts Way SO31 61 E3
Betteridge Dr SO16 28 B4
Beulah Rd SO16 43 E3
Bevan Cl SO19 59 F5
Beverley Gdns,
Bursledon SO31 60 D5
Beverley Gdns,
Romsey SO51 10 A4
Beverley Gdns,
Swanmore SO32 37 G5
Beverley Heights SO18 45 G1
Beverley Rd SO45 68 A2
Bevis Cl SO45 71 E2
Bevis Mews SO14 44 C5
Bevois St SO14 5 F3
Bevois Valley Rd SO14 5 F3
Biddenfield La SO32 50 C6
Bideford Cl SO16 42 B3
Bilberry Dr SO40 56 C4
Billington Gdns SO30 47 H2
Bindon Cl SO16 43 E2
Bindon Rd SO16 43 E2
Binsey Cl SO16 42 C4
Binstead Cl SO16 31 E5
Birch Cl, Romsey SO51 18 A2
Birch Cl,
Southampton SO16 43 E1
Birch Cl,
Winchester SO21 15 E5
Birch Gro SO50 21 G1
Birch Rd,
Chilworth SO16 30 B2

Birch Rd,
Hedge End SO30 47 H5
Birch Rd,
Southampton SO16 43 E1
Birchdale SO45 67 G5
Birchglade SO40 40 D2
Birchlands SO40 55 E1
Birchwood SO19 60 D1
Birchwood Gdns SO30 47 G3
Bishops Cl SO40 41 E4
Bishops Cres SO19 59 G2
Bishops Cl SO50 22 C2
Bishops La,
Bishops Waltham
SO32 36 B3
Bishops La,
Shirrell Heath SO32 51 G3
Bishops Rd SO19 59 F3
Bishops Wood Rd
SO32 51 G1
Bishopstoke La SO50 14 D6
Bishopstoke Mnr SO50 22 B5
Bishopstoke Rd SO50 22 A5
Bisley Ct SO19 60 A3
Bitterne Cres SO19 45 H6
Bitterne Village SO18 45 G5
Bitterne Rd,
Southampton SO18 45 E5
Bitterne Rd East SO18 46 A5
Bitterne Rd West SO18 45 E6
Blackberry Dr SO50 23 F6
Blackberry Ter SO14 44 C5
Blackbird Rd SO50 21 E6
Blackbushe Cl SO16 28 D5
Blackdown Cl SO45 66 D4
Blackfield Rd,
Blackfield SO45 70 D3
Blackfield Rd,
Fawley SO45 71 E2
Blackhorse La SO32 51 G3
Blackthorn Cl SO19 45 G6
Blackthorn Grn SO21 15 F5
Blackthorn Rd SO19 59 G1
Blackwater Dr SO40 40 D2
Blackwater Mews
SO40 40 D3
Bladon Rd SO16 43 G1
Blake Cl SO16 28 A5
Blakeney Rd SO16 42 B1
Blanchard Rd SO32 36 B2
Blann Cl SO16 28 A5
Bleaklow Cl SO16 42 D4
Blechynden Ter SO15 4 B2
Blencowe Dr SO53 20 A3
Blendworth La SO18 46 B5
Blenheim Av SO17 44 B3
Blenheim Cl,
Eastleigh SO53 20 A4
Blenheim Cl,
Southampton SO40 41 E6
Blenheim Gdns,
Dibden Purlieu SO45 66 C5
Blenheim Gdns,
Southampton SO17 44 C1
Blenheim Mews SO45 68 B2
Blenheim Rd SO50 21 H5
Blighmont Av SO15 43 F5
Blighmont Cres SO15 43 E5
Blind La,
Fareham PO17 72 C4
Blind La,
Southampton SO30 33 G5
Bloomsbury Walk
SO19 59 F4
Blossom Cl SO30 48 A5
Blue Anchor La SO14 4 D5
Bluebell Rd SO16 30 C5
Bluestar Gdns SO30 47 H1
Blundell La SO31 61 H5
Blyth Cl SO16 42 B2
Boakes Pl SO40 54 A3
Bodmin Rd SO50 22 D5
Bodycoats Rd SO53 21 E2
Bolderwood Cl SO50 22 D5
Bolderwood Rd SO16 29 H6
Bolhinton Av SO40 56 B5
Bonchurch Cl SO16 30 D5
Bond Rd SO18 45 F3
Bond St SO14 5 H1
Boniface Cl SO40 40 D4
Boniface Cres SO16 28 B6
Boothby Cl SO40 41 G6
Borrowdale Rd SO16 42 C4
Bossington Cl SO16 28 C4
Bosville SO50 21 H2
Boswell Cl,
Botley SO30 48 C5
Boswell Cl,
Southampton SO19 46 B6
Botany Bay Rd SO19 59 H4
Botley Gdns SO19 60 C3
Botley Hill SO30 48 D5
Botley Rd,
Bishops Waltham
SO32 36 A6
Botley Rd, Botley SO30 49 E5

Botley Rd,
Hedge End SO30 47 F3
Botley Rd,
Horton Heath SO50 23 H6
Botley Rd,
North Baddesley
SO52 18 B2
Botley Rd,
Romsey SO51 9 G6
Botley Rd,
Southampton SO19 60 A4
Botley Rd,
Swanick SO31 62 D6
Botley Rd,
West End SO30 46 D2
Botley Rd,
Whitenap SO51,52 18 A1
Bottings Ind Est
SO30 48 D5
Boundary Acre SO31 61 F2
Boundary Cl SO15 42 D5
Boundary Rd SO31 61 E6
Boundstone SO45 67 E4
Bourne Av SO15 43 G3
Bourne Cl SO21 14 A2
Bourne La,
Southampton SO40 53 F3
Bourne La,
Winchester SO21 7 F5
Bourne Rd,
Southampton SO15 4 A1
Bourne Rd,
Woodlands SO40 53 F4
Bournefields SO21 7 F5
Bournemouth Rd
SO53 20 D5
Bow La SO51 9 H6
Bowater Cl SO40 40 A6
Bowater Way SO40 40 A6
Bowcombe SO31 64 C1
Bowden La SO17 44 D2
Bower Cl,
Holbury SO45 70 B1
Bower Cl,
Southampton SO19 59 G5
Bowland Rise SO53 20 B1
Bowland Way SO45 70 D5
Bowman Ct SO19 60 A3
Boyatt Cres SO50 13 H5
Boyatt La SO50 13 H6
Boyes La SO21 15 F4
Boynton Cl SO53 12 C5
Bracken Cl SO52 19 E4
Bracken Cres SO50 23 E6
Bracken La SO16 43 E2
Bracken Pl SO16 30 B2
Bracken Rd SO52 19 E5
Brackenway Rd SO53 12 D5
Bracklesham Cl SO19 59 G3
Brackley Av SO50 23 G5
Brackley Way SO40 40 D3
Brading Cl SO16 31 E5
Bradley Grn SO16 42 B1
Bradshaw Cl SO50 24 A6
Braehead SO45 67 E4
Braeside Cl SO19 59 F1
Braeside Cres SO19 45 F6
Braeside Rd SO19 45 F6
Braishfield Cl SO16 42 D2
Braishfield Rd SO51 10 A5
Bramble Cl,
Eastleigh SO50 22 A3
Bramble Cl,
Southampton SO45 70 B1
Bramble Ct*,
Fairview Par SO45 67 F4
Bramble Dr SO45 10 A5
Bramble Hill SO53 20 C2
Bramble Mews SO18 45 H4
Bramblegate SO50 33 H1
Brambles Cl SO21 15 F6
Brambling Cl SO16 29 F4
Bramdean Rd SO18 46 C4
Bramley Cres SO19 60 A4
Bramley Gdns SO50 33 G3
Bramshott Hill SO45 66 A1
Bramshott Rd SO19 59 G6
Bramston Rd SO15 43 G4
Bramwell Ct*,
Bath Rd SO19 46 A6
Branksome Av SO15 43 G3
Bransbury Cl SO16 29 F5
Bransley Cl SO51 9 H4
Brasher Cl SO50 23 F5
Breamore Cl SO50 22 H1
Breamore Rd SO18 46 C5
Brean Cl SO16 42 C1
Brecon Cl,
Eastleigh SO53 20 C5
Brecon Cl,
Southampton SO45 66 D4
Brecon Rd SO19 46 A6
Brendon Cl SO45 66 C4
Brendon Grn SO16 42 D4
Brentwood Cres SO18 45 H3
Brewers La SO21 7 E6
Briar Ct SO45 67 F4

Briar Way SO16 10 A5
Briardene Ct SO40 41 E5
Briarswood SO16 43 F2
Briarswood Rise SO45 66 C4
Briarwood Rd SO40 40 C5
Brickfield La SO53 20 D3
Brickfield Rd SO17 44 D1
Brickfield Trading Est
SO53 20 D2
Brickmakers Rd SO21 15 E5
Brickwoods Cl SO51 9 H5
Brickyard Rd SO32 37 F6
Bridge Cl SO31 61 G5
Bridge Rd,
Bursledon SO31 61 F5
Bridge Rd,
Romsey SO51 9 G6
Bridge Rd,
Southampton SO19 59 E3
Bridge St PO17 72 D5
Bridge Ter,
Southampton SO14 5 G5
Bridge Ter,
Winchester SO21 6 D5
Bridgers Cl SO16 28 C4
Bridges Cl SO21 14 A2
Bridgwater Ct SO15 43 G6
Bridlington Av SO15 43 G3
Bridport Cl SO15 43 G6
Brighstone Cl SO16 30 D5
Brighton Rd SO15 44 B5
Brightside Rd SO16 42 D1
Brindle Cl SO16 30 C5
Brinton La SO45 67 F2
Brintons Rd SO14 5 E1
Brintons Ter SO14 44 C6
Britannia Gdns SO30 47 G1
Britannia Rd SO14 5 G2
Briton St SO14 4 D5
Broad Grn SO14 5 E2
Broad La,
North Baddesley
SO52 18 C2
Broad La,
Southampton SO14 5 E2
Broad La,
Swanmore SO32 37 F4
Broad Oak SO30 48 A5
Broadbent Cl SO16 28 B4
Broadlands Av SO50 21 H1
Broadlands Rd SO17 30 C6
Bradley Cl SO45 68 D6
Broadmead Rd SO16 28 B4
Broadmeadow Cl
SO40 41 E5
Broadoak Cl SO45 70 B1
Broadwalk Way SO40 56 D2
Broadwater Rd,
Romsey SO51 17 E1
Broadwater Rd,
Southampton SO18 45 G1
Broadway SO31 65 E3
Brockishill Rd SO40 52 C5
Brocks Cl SO45 66 C5
Brokenford Av SO40 41 G5
Brokenford La SO40 41 F5
Bromley Rd SO18 45 G3
Bronte Cl SO40 40 D5
Bronte Gdns PO15 63 E6
Bronte Way SO19 45 F6
Brook Cl SO52 19 E4
Brook Ct SO15 57 G1
Brook La SO30 48 B5
Brook Rd,
Eastleigh SO50 23 G6
Brook Rd,
Southampton SO18 45 H4
Brook St SO32 36 C2
Brook Valley SO16 42 D2
Brook Walk SO40 40 C3
Brook Way SO51 9 G4
Brookfield Rd SO50 23 G5
Brooklands SO32 36 C1
Brooklyn Cl SO21 14 B2
Brooklynn Cl SO32 50 D1
Brookside SO40 55 F1
Brookside Av SO15 42 D5
Brookside Way,
Southampton SO18 31 F5
Brookside Way,
West End SO30 46 D1
Brookvale Rd SO17 44 C3
Brookwood Av SO50 21 G5
Brookwood Ind Est
SO50 21 H4
Brookwood Rd SO16 42 B3
Broomhill Way SO16 21 H1
Brooms Gro SO19 60 C3
Broomy Cl SO45 66 C3
Broughton Cl SO16 43 E3
Brownhill Cl SO53 12 D6
Brownhill Ct SO16 42 C1
Brownhill Gdns SO53 13 E6
Brownhill Rd,
Eastleigh SO53 12 D6
Brownhill Rd,
Southampton SO52 19 E4

Brownhill Way SO16 42 A1
Browning Av SO19 46 C5
Browning Cl,
Eastleigh SO50 21 G4
Browning Cl,
Fareham PO15 63 E5
Browning Cl,
Southampton SO40 40 D5
Brownlow Av SO19 45 G6
Browning Gdns SO19 45 H6
Browsholme Cl SO50 21 H1
Broxburn Cl SO53 13 F5
Brue Cl SO53 20 C1
Brunel Cl SO30 48 A2
Brunel Rd,
Southampton SO15 42 A4
Brunel Rd,
Totton SO40 40 D1
Brunswick Cl SO50 23 F5
Brunswick Pl SO15 4 D1
Brunswick Rd SO50 23 G5
Brunswick Sq SO14 5 E5
Bryanston Rd SO19 59 E1
Bryony Gdns SO50 33 H3
Bubb La SO30 33 F6
Buchan Av PO15 63 E6
Buchan Ct SO45 66 C4
Buchanan Rd SO16 28 D4
Bucketts Farm Cl SO32 37 G4
Buckland Cl SO50 21 H2
Buckland Gdns SO40 40 C1
Buckley Cl SO16 43 F2
Buckthorn Cl SO40 40 B4
Buddens Rd PO17 72 C5
Budds La SO51 9 E5
Budds La Ind Est
SO51 9 E5
Bugle St SO14 4 D5
Bull La SO32 50 D1
Bullar Rd SO18 45 F5
Bullar St SO14 44 C6
Bullfinch Cl SO40 40 C4
Bullrush Cl SO45 67 G5
Bulls Copse Rd SO40 55 G2
Burbush Cl SO45 70 B1
Burgess Gdns SO16 43 H1
Burgess Rd SO16 30 B6
Burghclere Rd SO19 59 G6
Burgoyne Rd SO19 60 C2
Burke Dr SO19 46 B6
Burley Cl,
Eastleigh SO53 20 C4
Burley Cl,
Southampton SO40 40 B5
Burley Down SO53 20 C4
Burlington Ct SO19 60 A1
Burlington Rd SO15 44 A6
Burma Rd SO51 17 F1
Burma Way SO40 56 D5
Burnbank Gdns SO40 41 E5
Burnett Cl,
Southampton SO18 45 F3
Burnetts Flds SO50 33 H3
Burnetts Gdns SO50 33 H3
Burnetts La SO30,50 33 F6
Burnham Beeches
SO53 20 C2
Burnham Chase SO18 45 H4
Burns Cl SO50 21 F6
Burns Rd,
Eastleigh SO50 21 G6
Burns Rd,
Southampton SO19 46 C5
Burridge Rd SO31 62 C4
Bursledon Heights
SO31 61 F5
Bursledon Rd,
Hedge End SO30 61 F2
Bursledon Rd,
Southampton SO19 46 A6
Burton Rd SO15 44 A5
Bury La SO40 55 H1
Bury Rd SO40 56 B3
Busketts Way SO40 54 A4
Buttercup Cl,
Hedge End SO30 47 F5
Buttercup Cl,
Hythe SO45 67 F5
Buttercup Walk*,
Ibbotson Way SO40 55 E1
Butterfield Rd SO16 30 A6
Buttermere Cl SO16 42 C6
Butts Ash Av SO45 68 B2
Butts Ash Gdns SO45 68 B2
Butts Ash La SO45 68 A2
Butts Bridge Hill SO45 67 F4
Butts Bridge Rd SO45 67 F5
Butts Cl SO19 60 B2
Butts Cres SO19 60 B2
Butts Farm La SO32 36 D1
Butts Rd SO19 60 A4
Butts Sq SO19 60 B2
By The Wood SO40 40 D2
Byams La SO40 57 E4
Bye Rd SO31 62 A6

Cooks La, Romsey SO51 8 B2
Cooks La, Southampton SO40 40 C1
Coombe La SO51 8 A3
Cooper Rd SO40 54 C3
Coopers Cl SO18 46 B2
Coopers La SO19 59 F3
Copeland Rd SO16 42 B3
Copenhagen Twrs SO19 59 F6
Copinger Cl SO40 40 D6
Copperfield Rd SO16 30 B5
Copperfields SO40 40 C5
Coppice Hill SO32 36 C3
Coppice Rd SO40 40 D2
Copse Cl, Hythe SO45 67 E5
Copse Cl, North Baddesley SO52 18 D3
Copse Cl, Totton SO40 41 F6
Copse Cl, Winchester SO21 14 A1
Copse La, Hamble SO31 72 B1
Copse La, Southampton SO16 20 A6
Copse Rd SO18 45 G2
Copse Vw SO19 60 D1
Copsewood Rd, Ashurst SO40 54 C3
Copsewood Rd, Hythe SO45 67 E3
Copsewood Rd, Southampton SO18 45 F1
Copthorne La SO45 71 G1
Copythorne Cres SO40 39 F4
Corbiere Cl SO16 42 C1
Corbould Rd SO45 67 E6
Cordelia Cl SO45 66 D3
Coriander Dr SO40 40 C4
Coriander Way PO15 63 F6
Corinna Gdns SO45 66 D3
Corinthian Rd SO53 13 F6
Cork La SO40 56 D4
Cormorant Dr SO45 67 H4
Corn Hill SO32 36 D1
Cornel Rd SO19 59 G1
Cornfield Cl SO53 20 A2
Cornforth Rd SO40 40 D3
Cornmarket SO51 17 E1
Cornwall Cl SO18 45 G2
Cornwall Cres SO18 45 G2
Cornwall Rd, Eastleigh SO53 20 D4
Cornwall Rd, Southampton SO18 45 G2
Coronation Av SO15 44 A1
Coronation Par SO31 65 E5
Coronation Rd SO32 37 G5
Coronation Ter SO14 5 F3
Corsair Dr SO45 66 D3
Cortina Way SO30 61 H1
Cosford Cl SO50 23 F5
Cossack Grn SO14 5 E3
Cosworth Dr SO45 66 C4
Cotsalls SO50 33 H1
Cotswold Cl SO45 66 D4
Cotswold Rd SO16 42 D4
Cotton Cl SO50 22 C4
Coulsdon Rd SO30 47 G6
Coultas Rd SO53 13 F4
Court Cl, Calmore SO40 40 D1
Court Cl, Southampton SO18 45 H6
Court Rd SO15 44 A5
Court Royal Mews SO15 44 A4
Courtier Cl SO45 66 C3
Courtland Gdns SO16 30 C5
Coventry Rd SO15 44 A6
Cowdray Cl, Eastleigh SO50 23 E5
Cowdray Cl, Southampton SO16 29 F5
Cowley Cl SO16 42 C1
Cowper Rd SO19 46 C6
Cowslip Walk*, Ibbotson Way SO40 55 E1
Cowslip Way SO51 10 A5
Cox Row SO53 21 E4
Coxford Cl SO16 43 E2
Coxford Dro SO16 28 D6
Coxford Rd SO16 29 F6
Coxs Dr SO19 60 A4
Coxs Hill SO21 7 E3
Coxs La SO19 59 E3
Cozens Cl SO19 59 F5
Crabapple Cl SO40 40 C5
Crabbe La SO16 30 C5
Crabbs Way SO40 40 B5
Crabtree SO16 42 C2
Crabwood Cl SO16 42 C2
Crabwood Dr SO30 46 D3
Crabwood Rd SO16 42 C2
Cracknore Hard La SO40 57 E4
Cracknore Rd SO15 57 G1
Crampmoor La SO51 10 B5
Cranberry SO40 56 D5
Cranborne Gdns SO53 12 C5
Cranbourne Cl SO15 43 H3
Cranbourne Dr SO21 14 A3
Cranbourne Pk SO30 61 G1
Cranbury Av SO14 44 C5
Cranbury Cl SO21 14 A3
Cranbury Gdns SO31 60 D5
Cranbury Pl SO14 44 B6
Cranbury Rd, Eastleigh SO50 21 H6
Cranbury Rd, Southampton SO19 59 G3
Cranbury Ter SO14 44 B5
Cranford Gdns SO53 12 C5
Cranford Way SO17 44 C2
Cranleigh Rd SO30 47 H6
Cranmer Dr SO16 28 A5
Cranmore SO31 64 C1
Cranwell Ct SO16 28 D5
Craven Rd SO53 21 E2
Craven St SO14 5 E2
Craven Walk SO14 5 E2
Crawford Cl SO16 28 B4
Crawte Av SO45 70 C2
Creedy Gdns SO18 45 H1
Creighton Rd SO15 42 D5
Crescent Rd SO52 18 D3
Cressey Rd SO51 17 F1
Crest Way SO19 60 B2
Crete Cotts SO45 67 E6
Crete La SO45 67 E6
Crete Rd SO45 67 E6
Cricklemede SO32 36 D3
Cricklewood Cl SO32 36 D2
Crigdon Cl SO16 42 C3
Crispin Cl SO50 33 G4
Crofton Cl SO17 44 B2
Crofton Way SO32 37 F5
Cromalt Cl SO45 66 C4
Cromarty Rd SO16 28 C5
Cromer Rd SO16 42 B3
Cromwell Rd SO15 44 A5
Crooked Hays Cl SO40 56 D5
Crookham Rd SO19 59 G5
Cross La SO32 25 H4
Cross Rd SO19 45 F5
Cross St SO32 36 C2
Crosshouse Rd SO14 5 G5
Crossley Ct SO15 43 G5
Crossways SO21 6 C6
Crosswell Cl SO19 60 B1
Crowders Grn SO21 15 E5
Crown St SO15 43 F3
Crowsnest La SO32 48 B3
Crowsport Est SO31 65 G5
Crowther Cl SO19 60 B2
Croydon Cl SO16 29 E5
Crummock Rd SO53 12 B6
Crusader Rd SO30 47 H6
Crusaders Way SO53 20 A2
Cuckmere La SO16 42 A4
Cuckoo Bushes La SO53 12 D5
Cuckoo La SO14 4 D5
Cudworth Mead SO30 47 H3
Culford Av SO40 41 F5
Culford Way SO40 41 F5
Culver SO31 64 C1
Culver Cl SO16 42 B2
Culverlands Cl SO32 51 E5
Culvery Gdns SO18 45 H2
Cumberland Av SO53 21 F2
Cumberland Cl SO53 21 F2
Cumberland Pl SO15 4 C1
Cumberland St SO14 5 F3
Cumberland Way SO45 66 C3
Cumbrian Way SO16 42 C4
Cummins Grn SO31 61 E5
Cunard Av SO15 43 G4
Cunard Rd SO14 5 E6
Cunningham Av SO32 36 A1
Cunningham Cres SO19 60 A2
Cunningham Gdns SO31 60 D6
Cupernham Cl SO51 9 G5
Cupernham La SO51 9 G2
Curdridge La SO32 50 A2
Curlew Cl, Hythe SO45 67 H5
Curlew Cl, Southampton SO16 29 F5
Curlew Dr SO45 67 G4
Curlew Sq SO50 21 F6
Curlew Walk SO45 67 G4
Curzon Ct SO16 29 G6
Cutbush La SO18 46 A3
Cygnus Gdns SO45 66 B3
Cypress Av SO19 59 G1
Cypress Gdns, Botley SO30 48 C5
Cypress Gdns, Totton SO40 40 C5
Cyprus Av SO40 54 D3
D Avenue SO45 69 E4
Daffodil Rd SO16 31 E5
Dahlia Rd SO16 30 C6
Daintree Cl SO19 60 C3
Dairy La SO16 27 G5
Dairymoor PO17 72 C5
Daisy Rd SO16 30 D6
Dale Grn SO53 12 C5
Dale Rd, Hythe SO45 67 E3
Dale Rd, Southampton SO16 43 F2
Dale Valley Cl SO16 43 F2
Dale Valley Gdns SO16 43 G1
Dale Valley Rd SO16 43 F2
Dales Way SO40 40 C4
Damen Cl SO30 61 F1
Damson Cres SO50 23 F6
Damson Hill SO32 37 G2
Dane Cl SO45 71 E4
Danebury Gdns SO53 20 B4
Danebury Way SO16 28 B6
Daniels Walk SO40 40 C3
Dapple Pl SO40 56 D5
Dark La SO45 70 D3
Darlington Gdns SO15 43 G3
Dart Rd SO18 45 H1
Dartington Rd SO50 22 C3
Darwin Rd, Eastleigh SO50 22 A3
Darwin Rd, Southampton SO15 43 H5
David Ct SO51 17 G1
Davidson Cl SO45 67 G2
Dawlish Av SO15 43 G3
Dawnay Cl SO16 31 E5
Dawson Rd SO19 60 B4
Dayrell Cl SO40 40 C3
De Grouchy La SO17 44 B2
Deacon Cl SO19 45 H6
Deacon Cres SO19 45 H6
Deacon Rd SO19 45 H6
Dean Ct SO30 47 G5
Dean Rd, Eastleigh SO50 33 G1
Dean Rd, Southampton SO18 45 H4
Deanfield Cl SO31 65 F6
Deansfield Cl SO51 9 H5
Dee Cl SO53 20 C2
Deeping Cl SO19 59 G5
Deer Park Fm Ind Est SO50 24 A6
Deerhurst Cl SO40 40 D6
Deerleap Cl SO45 67 F4
Deerleap La SO40 54 D3
Deerleap Way SO45 67 F4
Defender Rd SO19 59 E2
Defender Walk SO19 59 E3
Delius Av SO19 60 C3
Dell Cl SO50 23 G6
Dell Rd SO18 45 G2
Dempsey Cl SO19 60 A2
Denbigh Cl, Eastleigh SO50 21 G2
Denbigh Cl, Southampton SO40 54 D1
Denbigh Gdns SO16 30 B5
Dene Cl SO16 30 A3
Dene Rd SO40 54 C4
Dene Way SO40 54 C3
Denewulf Cl SO32 36 C1
Denham Flds SO50 23 G4
Denham Gdns SO31 64 B3
Denmead Rd SO18 46 B4
Denny Cl SO45 71 F1
Denny Lodge Walk SO45 68 B3
Denzil Av, Netley SO31 64 C2
Denzil Av, Southampton SO14 44 C5
Depedene Cl SO45 70 A1
Derby Rd, Eastleigh SO50 21 F6
Derby Rd, Southampton SO14 5 F2
Deridene Ct SO40 40 D6
Derwent Cl SO18 46 A3
Derwent Dr SO40 40 C4
Derwent Rd SO16 42 C3
Desborough Rd SO50 21 H6
Devine Gdns SO50 22 C5
Devon Cl SO53 20 D4
Devon Dr SO53 20 D4
Devonshire Gdns, Bursledon SO31 61 E4
Devonshire Gdns, Hythe SO45 68 B2
Devonshire Rd SO15 4 C1
Dew La SO50 21 G5
Dibben Walk SO51 10 A4
Dibble Dr SO52 18 D4
Dibden Lodge Cl SO45 67 E2
Dickens Dell SO40 40 B5
Dickens Dr PO15 63 E5
Dickson Pk PO17 72 D4
Didcot Rd SO15 43 F3
Diligence Cl SO31 61 E5
Dimond Cl SO18 45 F2
Dimond Hill SO18 45 F3
Dimond Rd SO18 45 F1
Dodds La SO32 37 G5
Dodwell La SO31 61 F3
Dolphin Cl SO50 23 E6
Dolphin Ct SO50 23 E6
Dolphin Hill SO21 7 E6
Dolton Rd SO16 28 D6
Dominy Cl SO45 67 G2
Doncaster Dro SO50 31 F2
Doncaster Rd SO50 31 H2
Donigers Cl SO32 37 F3
Donigers Dell SO32 37 G4
Donkey La SO30 48 D5
Donnington Dr SO53 20 C4
Donnington Gro SO17 44 D2
Doric Cl SO53 13 G6
Dorland Gdns SO40 40 D6
Dorset Rd SO53 20 D4
Dorset St SO14 5 E1
Douglas Cres SO19 46 B5
Douglas Way SO45 67 E2
Dove Dale SO50 21 E6
Dover St SO14 44 B5
Dowds Cl SO30 47 G4
Downland Cl SO30 48 B5
Downland Pl SO30 61 F1
Downs Park Av SO40 41 G6
Downs Park Cres SO40 41 G6
Downs Park Rd SO40 41 G6
Downscroft Gdns SO30 47 F5
Downside Av SO19 45 H6
Downton Rd SO18 45 G2
Downwood Cl SO45 66 C5
Doyle Ct SO19 59 G5
Dragoon Cl SO19 60 B2
Drake Cl SO40 56 D4
Drake Rd SO50 22 C4
Drakes Cl SO45 67 E4
Drayton Cl SO19 59 G6
Drayton Pl SO40 41 E5
Driftwood Gdns SO40 40 C5
Drinkwater Cl SO50 21 G4
Drove Cl SO21 7 E6
Drove Rd SO19 60 A1
Droxford Rd, Fareham PO17 72 D5
Droxford Rd, Southampton SO32 37 H5
Drummond Dr SO17 44 D4
Drummond Rd, Hedge End SO30 47 G3
Drummond Rd, Hythe SO45 67 F2
Drummond Way SO53 12 C5
Dryden Rd SO19 60 D1
Duddon Cl SO18 46 A2
Duke Rd SO30 47 H6
Duke St SO14 5 F4
Dukes Mill Shopping Centre SO51 17 E1
Dukes Rd SO17 44 D4
Dukeswood Dr SO45 67 F5
Dumbleton Cl SO19 61 E1
Dumpers Dro SO50 33 H3
Dunbar Cl SO16 28 D5
Dunbridge La SO51 8 A1
Duncan Cl SO19 59 F5
Duncan Ct SO19 60 B2
Dundee Rd SO17 44 D3
Dundonald Cl SO19 59 E5
Dundridge La SO32 36 D1
Dundry Way SO30 47 H4
Dunfield Copse SO45 71 E2
Dunkirk Cl SO16 29 G5
Dunkirk Rd SO16 29 G6
Dunnings La SO52 18 C3
Dunster Cl SO16 29 G4
Dunvegan Dr SO16 29 F4
Durban Cl SO51 9 G5
Durley Brook Rd SO32 34 B4
Durley Cres SO40 55 E1
Durley Hall La SO32 24 D6
Durley Rd SO50 34 A2
Durley St SO32 35 E3
Durlston Rd SO16 42 A3
Durnford Rd SO14 5 F1
Dutton La SO50 22 A4
Duttons Rd SO51 9 E5
Dyer Rd SO15 43 G5
Dymott Cl SO15 43 G6
Dyneley Grn SO18 45 H2
Dyram Cl SO50 21 G3
Dyserth Cl SO19 60 A5
Eadens La SO40 53 G1
Eagle Cl SO53 20 C3
Earls Cl SO50 23 F6
Earls Rd SO14 44 C4
East Avenue SO45 69 F5
East Bargate SO14 4 D4
East Dr SO50 22 C4
East Park Ter SO14 5 E1
East Rd SO45 69 E2
East St SO14 4 D4
East St Centre SO14 58 B2
East St Shopping Centre SO14 5 E4
Eastbourne Av SO15 43 H4
Eastchurch Cl SO16 28 D6
Eastcot Cl SO45 70 B1
Eastern Rd SO30 46 C3
Eastfield Rd SO17 45 E4
Eastgate St SO14 4 D4
Eastleigh Rd SO50 23 G6
Eastmeare Ct SO40 40 C6
Eastville SO50 23 H6
Eastways SO32 36 C2
Eastwood Ct SO51 17 F1
Eddystone Rd SO40 40 D1
Edelvale Rd SO18 46 A3
Eden Rd SO18 46 A1
Eden Walk SO53 20 C3
Edgehill Rd SO18 45 G3
Edington Cl SO32 36 B1
Edith Haisman Cl SO15 4 A1
Edmunds Cl SO30 62 A1
Edward Av SO50 22 C3
Edward Cl SO45 70 D3
Edward Rd, Hythe SO45 67 F2
Edward Rd, Southampton SO15 43 F5
Edwin Jones Grn SO15 44 A4
Edwina Cl, North Baddesley SO52 19 E3
Edwina Cl, Southampton SO19 45 G6
Effingham Gdns SO19 60 B2
Eight Acres SO51 9 H6
Eighth St SO45 69 E6
Elan Cl SO18 46 A2
Elder Cl SO40 56 D4
Elder Grn SO21 15 F6
Elderberry Cl SO50 23 F6
Eldridge Gdns SO51 9 F5
Electron Way SO53 20 D2
Eleventh St SO45 69 E5
Elgar Cl SO19 60 B3
Elgar Rd SO19 60 B3
Elgin Cl SO45 67 G4
Elgin Rd SO15 57 G1
Eling Hill SO40 41 H6
Eling La SO40 41 G5
Elizabeth Cl SO30 46 C3
Elizabeth Gdns SO45 67 F5
Elizabeth Rd PO17 72 C5
Elizabeth Way, Eastleigh SO50 22 A3
Elizabeth Way, Southampton SO32 36 A2
Elland Cl SO50 33 H1
Elldene Ct SO40 41 E6
Ellen Gdns SO53 20 C3
Elliot Cl SO40 40 D5
Elliot Mews SO30 47 H2
Elliot Rise SO30 47 H2
Ellis Rd SO19 60 D1
Ellwood Av SO19 46 D6
Ellwood Cl SO19 46 D6
Elm Cl SO16 30 B6
Elm Cres, Hythe SO45 68 B3
Elm Cres, Upham SO32 25 G2
Elm Gdns SO30 46 C1
Elm Gro SO50 21 G6
Elm Rd SO32 36 D2
Elm St SO14 5 G4
Elm Ter SO14 5 G4
Elmes Dr SO15 42 D5
Elmsleigh Ct SO16 30 B6
Elmsleigh Gdns SO16 30 B6
Elmslie Gdns SO31 60 D5
Elmtree Cl SO40 54 C4
Elmtree Gdns, Eastleigh SO50 21 H6
Elmtree Gdns, Romsey SO51 18 A1
Elmwood Ct SO16 43 F2
Elstree Rd SO19 59 F1
Embley Cl SO40 40 D2
Embsay Rd SO31 61 H6
Emer Cl SO52 19 E2
Emerald Cl SO19 45 H6
Emerald Cres SO45 67 G2
Emmett Rd SO16 28 D5
Emmons Cl SO31 72 B2
Empress Pk SO14 44 C5
Empress Rd SO14 44 C5
Emsworth Rd SO15 43 F4
Endeavour Cl SO15 43 F4
Endeavour Way SO45 67 F1
Enderwood Cl SO40 40 C4
Endle St SO14 5 G4
Enfield Gro SO19 59 F3
Englefield Rd SO18 45 E4
English Rd SO15 43 F5

Grenville Ct SO15 44 A5
Grenville Gdns SO45 67 F6
Gresley Gdns SO30 47 H2
Greville Rd SO15 43 H4
Greyhound Cl SO30 47 G1
Greywell Av SO16 29 F6
Griffin Cl SO50 22 C5
Griffin Ct SO17 45 E4
Griffin Ind Pk SO40 41 E1
Griffon Cl SO31 61 E4
Grosvenor Cl SO17 44 D2
Grosvenor Gdns,
Southampton SO17 44 D2
Grosvenor Gdns,
West End SO30 46 C3
Grosvenor Mews
SO17 44 D2
Grosvenor Rd,
Eastleigh SO53 13 F5
Grosvenor Rd,
Southampton SO17 44 D2
Grosvenor Sq SO15 4 C1
Grove Copse SO19 60 A5
Grove Ct SO31 64 D1
Grove Gdns SO19 60 A4
Grove Pl SO19 60 A4
Grove Rd,
Southampton SO15 43 F5
Grove Rd,
Winchester SO21 14 B1
Grove St SO14 5 F4
Grovely Way SO51 10 C4
Guernsey Cl SO16 28 C6
Guest Rd SO50 22 C5
Guildford Dr SO53 20 C4
Guildford St SO14 5 G2
Guildhall Sq SO14 4 D2
Guillemot Cl SO45 67 G4
Gullycroft Mead SO30 47 F5
Gunners Pk SO32 36 D2
Gurney Rd SO15 43 G4
Gypsy Gro SO15 43 G5

Hack Dr SO21 15 E6
Hackworth Gdns
SO30 47 G1
Haddon Dr SO50 21 H2
Hadleigh Gdns SO50 21 H2
Hadley Fld SO45 68 C5
Hadrian Way SO16 30 A3
Hadrians Cl SO53 21 F1
Haflinger Dr PO15 62 D6
Haig Rd SO50 23 F6
Haileybury Gdns
SO30 47 G3
Halden Cl SO51 9 H4
Hales Dr SO30 61 F1
Hall Cl SO32 36 D2
Hall Lands La SO50 24 A6
Hallett Cl SO18 45 H2
Halstead Rd SO18 45 G2
Halterworth Cl SO51 9 H6
Halterworth La SO51 10 A6
Haltons Cl SO40 40 D3
Hambert Way SO40 41 E6
Hamble Ct SO53 21 E2
Hamble House Gdns
SO31 65 F6
Hamble La SO31 60 D6
Hamble Manor Ct
SO31 72 C1
Hamble Springs SO32 36 D3
Hamble Wood SO30 48 D6
Hambleside Ct SO31 72 B1
Hameldon Cl SO16 42 C4
Hamilton Mews SO45 67 G5
Hamilton Rd,
Eastleigh SO50 22 C4
Hamilton Rd,
Southampton SO45 68 C2
Hammonds Cl SO40 41 E4
Hammonds Grn SO40 40 D3
Hammonds La SO40 41 E4
Hammonds Way SO40 41 E3
Hampshire
Corporate Pk SO53 20 C5
Hampton Cl SO45 70 D4
Hampton Gdns SO45 70 D4
Hampton Hill SO32 37 G4
Hampton La SO45 70 D2
Hampton Twrs SO19 59 F6
Hamtun Cres SO40 41 F3
Hamtun Gdns SO40 41 E3
Hamtun Rd SO19 60 A3
Hamtun St SO14 4 D4
Handel Rd SO15 4 C1
Handel Ter SO15 4 C1
Handford Pl SO15 44 B6
Hanley Rd SO15 43 H4
Hann Rd SO16 28 C3
Hannay Rise SO19 60 C1
Hanns Way SO50 21 H5
Hanover Bldgs SO14 5 E4
Hanover Buildings
SO14 4 D3
Harborough Rd SO15 44 A6
Harbour Par SO15 4 C3
Harbourne Gdns SO18 46 A2
Harcourt Rd SO18 45 F4
Harding La SO50 23 F4
Hardley La SO45 68 C3
Hardwick Rd SO53 21 E2
Hardwicke Cl SO16 42 D2
Hardwicke Way SO31 64 D6
Hardy Cl SO15 43 F6
Hardy Dr SO45 67 G5
Hardy Rd SO50 21 G6
Hare La SO21 15 E1
Harefield Ct SO51 9 H5
Harefield Rd SO17 30 D6
Harewood Cl SO50 21 H2
Harland Cres SO15 43 G3
Harlaxton Cl SO50 21 G2
Harlech Dr SO53 20 B3
Harlyn Rd SO16 42 D3
Harold Cl SO40 40 D5
Harold Rd SO15 43 G5
Harrier Cl SO16 29 E4
Harrier Grn SO45 68 C4
Harrier Way SO45 68 C4
Harris Av SO30 47 G4
Harrison Cut SO14 5 F3
Harrison Rd SO17 30 D6
Harrisons Cut SO15 43 F3
Hart Hill SO45 67 H5
Hartington Rd SO14 5 G1
Hartley Av SO17 44 C1
Hartley Cl,
Eastleigh SO50 23 E6
Hartley Cl,
Southampton SO45 67 F6
Hartley Ct SO16 30 B5
Hartley Rd SO50 23 E6
Hartley Walk SO45 67 F5
Hartsgrove Av SO45 70 D3
Hartsgrove Cl SO45 70 D3
Harvest Rd SO53 20 A2
Harvey Ct SO45 70 D2
Harvey Gdns SO45 67 G3
Harvey Rd SO50 22 C5
Harwood Cl SO40 41 E4
Haselbury Rd SO40 41 F5
Haselfoot Gdns SO30 46 C4
Hatch Mead SO30 46 B2
Hatchley La SO32 24 D2
Hathaway Cl SO50 22 A4
Hatherell Cl SO30 46 B3
Hatley Rd SO18 45 H4
Havelock Rd SO14 4 C2
Havendale SO30 61 H1
Havenstone Way SO18 31 F5
Havre Twrs SO19 59 F6
Haweswater Cl SO16 42 C2
Hawfinch Cl SO16 29 F4
Hawkeswood Rd
SO18 44 D5
Hawkhill SO45 66 B3
Hawkhurst Cl SO19 59 H5
Hawkley Grn SO19 59 G5
Hawthorn Cl,
Eastleigh SO50 23 G6
Hawthorn Cl,
Southampton SO30 48 A5
Hawthorn Cl,
Winchester SO21 15 E5
Hawthorn Rd,
Hythe SO45 67 E3
Hawthorn Rd,
Southampton SO17 44 B1
Hawthorne Rd SO40 41 E4
Hayburn Rd SO16 42 B2
Haydock Cl SO40 40 D4
Hayes Mead SO45 68 C5
Hayle Rd SO18 46 A1
Hayley Cl SO45 68 B2
Haynes Rd SO18 45 H5
Haynes Way SO45 66 D5
Hayter Gdns SO51 9 G6
Hayward Cl SO40 40 D4
Hayward Ct SO45 68 D6
Hazel Cl,
Eastleigh SO53 12 D4
Hazel Cl,
Winchester SO21 15 E5
Hazel Farm Rd SO40 40 C5
Hazel Gro SO40 54 A3
Hazel Rd SO19 59 E2
Hazeldown Rd SO16 28 C4
Hazeleigh Av SO19 59 F4
Hazeley Rd SO21 7 E6
Hazelwood Rd SO18 45 H3
Hearne Gdns SO32 51 G3
Heath Cl SO50 23 H6
Heath Gdns SO31 64 D1
Heath House Cl SO30 61 G2
Heath House Gdns
SO30 61 G2
Heath House La SO30 61 G2
Heath Rd,
North Baddesley SO52 19 E4
Heath Rd,
Southampton SO19 59 H1
Heathcote Rd SO53 21 E2
Heathen St SO32 34 C6
Heather Chase SO50 23 F6
Heather Cl SO40 41 E5
Heather Ct SO18 46 B5
Heather Rd SO45 71 E2
Heatherbrae Gdns
SO52 18 D4
Heatherdeane Rd SO17 44 B2
Heatherdene Rd SO53 13 F5
Heatherlands Rd SO16 30 A2
Heatherstone Av SO45 67 E6
Heatherview Cl SO52 18 D2
Heathfield SO45 67 E4
Heathfield Cl,
Eastleigh SO53 13 E4
Heathfield Cl,
Southampton SO19 60 A3
Heathfield Rd,
Eastleigh SO53 13 E4
Heathfield Rd,
Southampton SO19 60 A3
Heathlands SO32 51 E5
Heathlands Cl SO53 12 D6
Heathlands Rd SO53 12 D6
Hedge End
Bsns Centre SO30 47 G3
Hedge End
Retail Pk SO30 47 F5
Hedgerow Cl SO16 28 C3
Hedgerow Dr SO18 46 A3
Hedley Cl SO45 71 E3
Hedley Gdns SO30 47 G1
Heinz Burt Cl SO50 21 G5
Helford Gdns SO18 45 H2
Helvellyn Rd SO16 42 C4
Hemdean Gdns SO30 46 C3
Hemingway Gdns
PO15 63 E6
Hemlock Way SO53 20 A3
Hemming Cl SO40 41 F6
Henry Cl SO45 68 C4
Henry Rd,
Eastleigh SO50 22 C3
Henry Rd,
Southampton SO15 43 F5
Henry St SO15 44 A6
Henstead Rd SO15 44 A6
Hensting La,
Eastleigh SO50 23 G1
Hensting La,
Winchester SO21 15 G6
Henty Rd SO16 43 E4
Hepworth Cl SO19 60 B4
Herald Ind Est SO30 47 G3
Herald Rd SO30 47 F3
Herbert Walker Av SO15 4 A3
Hereward Cl SO51 9 H6
Hermitage Cl SO32 36 A1
Heron Sq SO50 21 F6
Herons Wood SO40 40 D2
Herrick Cl SO19 60 C2
Hestia Cl SO51 10 A5
Hewitts Rd SO15 4 A2
Heyes Dr SO19 60 B3
Heysham Rd SO15 43 F4
Heywood Grn SO19 60 D1
Hickory Gdns SO30 46 B1
High Firs Gdns SO51 10 A6
High Firs Rd,
Romsey SO51 10 A6
High Firs Rd,
Southampton SO19 60 A1
High Mdw SO19 46 B6
High Rd SO16 31 E6
High St,
Bishops Waltham
SO32 36 C2
High St, Botley SO30 48 B5
High St,
Bursledon SO31 65 G1
High St,
Eastleigh SO50 31 H1
High St, Hamble SO31 65 F6
High St, Hythe SO45 67 F2
High St, Shirley SO15 43 F4
High St,
Shirrel Heath SO32 51 E5
High St,
Southampton SO14 4 D4
High St, Totton SO40 41 G5
High St, Twyford SO21 7 E6
High St,
West End SO30 46 B2
High Trees SO50 24 B5
Highbridge Rd,
Eastleigh SO50 14 C6
Highbridge Rd,
Winchester SO21 15 E4
Highbury Cl SO50 33 G1
Highclere Rd SO16 29 H6
Highclere Way SO53 20 C4
Highcliff Av SO14 44 B4
Highcliffe Dr SO50 21 H1
Highcrown Mews
SO17 44 B1
Highcrown St SO17 44 B2
Highfield SO21 7 E6
Highfield Av,
Southampton SO17 44 B1
Highfield Av,
Winchester SO21 7 F6
Highfield Cl,
Eastleigh SO53 21 F2
Highfield Cl,
Southampton SO17 44 C2
Highfield Cres SO17 44 C2
Highfield La SO17 44 B1
Highfield Rd,
Eastleigh SO53 21 F2
Highfield Rd,
Southampton SO17 44 B2
Highgrove Cl SO40 55 E1
Highlands Cl,
Dibden Purlieu SO45 67 F5
Highlands Cl,
North Baddesley
SO52 18 C2
Highlands Way SO45 67 F5
Highview Way SO18 45 G3
Highways Rd SO21 6 B6
Highwood La SO51 10 A5
Hill Cl SO50 23 G3
Hill Farm Rd SO15 43 H6
Hill La,
Southampton SO15 4 B1
Hill La,
Winchester SO21 15 E5
Hill Pl SO31 61 F5
Hill Pound SO32 37 G6
Hill Rise SO21 7 E6
Hill St SO40 26 C4
Hillcrest Av SO53 21 E2
Hillcrest Cl SO52 18 C3
Hillcrest Dr SO53 21 E2
Hillcrest Gdns SO32 36 D6
Hilldene Way SO30 46 C3
Hilldown Rd SO17 44 C1
Hillgrove Rd SO18 45 G1
Hillside SO32 49 H4
Hillside Av,
Romsey SO51 9 H6
Hillside Av,
Southampton SO18 45 F3
Hillside Cl SO53 21 E1
Hillsons Rd SO30 49 E5
Hilltop Dr SO19 60 B2
Hillview Rd SO45 67 E3
Hillyfields SO16 28 A6
Hiltingbury Cl SO53 13 E5
Hiltingbury Rd SO53 12 C4
Hilton Rd SO30 47 H5
Hinkler Rd SO19 46 C5
Hinton Cres SO19 60 D1
Hirst Rd SO45 67 G4
Hispano Av PO15 63 E6
Hoads Hill PO17 72 D6
Hobart Dr SO45 67 G3
Hobb La SO30 47 H5
Hobson Way SO45 70 B1
Hockley Link SO21 6 D2
Hocombe Dr SO53 12 C3
Hocombe Park Cl SO53 12 D3
Hocombe Rd SO53 12 C3
Hocombe Wood Rd
SO53 12 C4
Hodder Cl SO53 20 C2
Hoe La,
Mountbatten Park
SO51,52 18 A5
Hoe La, Romsey SO51 17 H5
Hoe Rd SO32 36 D2
Hogarth Cl,
Romsey SO51 9 H5
Hogarth Cl,
Southampton SO19 60 A3
Hogwood La SO30 32 C4
Holbury Dro SO45 68 D6
Holcroft Rd SO19 46 D6
Hole La SO32 49 H2
Holkham Cl SO16 42 C1
Holland Cl SO53 20 D4
Holland Pl SO16 43 E2
Holland Rd,
Southampton SO19 59 E4
Holland Rd,
Totton SO40 40 C5
Hollingbourne Cl SO18 45 E4
Hollman Dr SO51 9 E6
Holly Cl SO45 68 B3
Holly Dell SO16 30 A5
Holly Gdns SO30 46 C1
Holly Hatch Rd SO40 41 E5
Holly Hill SO16 30 A5
Holly Hill Cl SO16 30 A5
Holly Lodge SO53 20 D5
Holly Oak Ct SO16 29 E6
Holly Oak Rd SO16 29 E6
Holly Rd,
Ashurst SO40 54 B4
Holly Rd,
Blackfield SO45 70 D5
Hollybank Cl SO45 67 F3
Hollybank Cres SO45 67 F2
Hollybank Rd SO45 67 E3
Hollybrook Av SO16 43 G1
Hollybrook Cl SO16 43 F2
Hollybrook Rd SO16 43 G1
Hollywood Cl SO52 18 C3
Holmes Cl SO31 64 B2
Holmesland Dr SO30 48 B5
Holmesland La SO30 48 B5
Holmesland Walk*,
Holmesland La SO30 48 B5
Holmsley Cl SO18 46 B5
Holmsley Ct SO40 40 C4
Holt Cl PO17 72 C5
Holt Ct SO19 59 F6
Holt Rd SO15 44 A5
Holyborne Rd SO51 9 H6
Holyrood Av SO17 44 C2
Holyrood Pl SO14 4 D5
Home Farm Cl SO45 67 G4
Home Field Dr SO16 28 A4
Home Fld SO51 9 G4
Homer Farm La SO45 70 D6
Honeysuckle Rd SO16 30 C6
Honeysuckle Way
SO53 20 B1
Honeywood Cl SO40 41 E3
Honister Cl SO16 42 C4
Hood Rd SO18 45 H4
Hook Cl SO51 12 B4
Hook Cres SO51 12 B3
Hook Rd SO51 12 B3
Hookwater Cl SO53 12 C3
Hookwater Rd SO53 12 C3
Hookwood La SO51 12 A3
Hope Rd SO30 46 C2
Horder Cl SO16 30 A6
Hornbeam Cl SO30 48 A5
Hornbeam Gdns SO30 46 C1
Hornbeam Rd SO53 20 A2
Hornchurch Rd SO16 28 D5
Horns Dro SO16 28 B4
Horns Hill SO16 28 B3
Horns Hill Cl SO16 28 B4
Horsebridge Way
SO16 28 C4
Horsecroft SO51 9 F5
Horsefair Ct SO51 9 E6
Horsefair Mews SO51 9 E6
Horseshoe Dr,
Romsey SO51 9 H4
Horseshoe Dr,
Southampton SO40 40 A2
Horton Way SO50 22 D6
Hospital Rd SO32 51 F3
Hotspur Cl SO45 67 E2
Houchin St SO32 36 C2
Hound Cl SO31 64 D3
Hound Rd SO31 64 D3
Hound Road Gdns
SO31 64 D2
Hound Way SO31 64 C2
Houndwell Pl SO14 5 E4
Hounsdown Av SO40 55 F1
Hounsdown Bsns Pk
SO40 55 F2
Hounsdown Cl SO40 55 F1
Hoveton Gro SO53 12 C6
Howard Cl,
Chandler's Ford SO53 21 F3
Howard Cl,
Fair Oak SO50 23 G6
Howard Cl,
Southampton SO18 31 F5
Howard Rd SO15 43 H5
Howards Gro SO15 43 F4
Hoyle Cl SO32 25 F4
Hudson Ct SO40 40 D6
Hughes Cl SO45 70 D3
Hulles Way SO52 18 D4
Hulse Rd SO15 44 A4
Hulse Way SO15 44 A4
Hulton Cl SO19 59 E5
Humber Gdns SO31 61 E5
Hungerford SO31 61 E6
Hunt Av SO31 64 C2
Hunter Cl SO45 68 C4
Hunters Cres,
Romsey SO51 10 A4
Hunters Cres,
Southampton SO40 40 C6
Hunters Ct SO31 61 F2
Hunters Hill SO40 55 E3
Hunters Way SO50 23 E6
Huntingdon Cl SO40 41 E2
Huntingdon Gdns
SO50 34 A3
Huntly Way SO18 45 G5
Hunton Cl SO16 43 G1
Hunts La SO21 6 D5
Huntsman Rd SO31 72 C3
Hurdle Way SO21 6 A4
Hurlingham Gdns
SO16 30 C5
Hurricane Dr SO16 28 C3
Hursley Dr SO45 70 D5
Hursley Rd SO53 12 C2
Hurst Cl,
Eastleigh SO53 20 C4
Hurst Cl,

Southampton SO40 41 G4
Hurst Green Cl SO19 59 H5
Hurst La SO50 24 C1
Hurstbourne Pl SO19 59 G6
Hutwood Rd SO16 30 B1
Huxley Ct SO45 66 C4
Hyde Cl,
  Southampton SO15 43 F3
Hyde Cl, Totton SO40 40 C5
Hyman Way SO40 41 F5
Hythe By-Pass SO45 66 A1
Hythe Rd SO40 56 C5

Ibbotson Way SO40 55 E1
Ibsen Cl PO15 63 E6
Imber Way SO19 60 B2
Imperial Av SO15 44 C5
Imperial Rd SO14 44 C5
Imperial Way SO15 57 F1
Ingersley Rise SO30 46 C3
Ingle Glen SO45 67 F5
Ingle Grn SO40 40 C3
Ingleside SO31 64 C1
Ingleton Rd SO16 42 B3
Inglewood Gdns SO50 23 G5
Ingram Ct SO17 45 E4
Inkerman Rd SO19 59 E3
Inner Av SO14 44 B5
International Way SO19 13 G6
Ionic Cl SO53 13 G6
Ipley Way SO45 67 F5
Iris Rd SO16 30 C6
Irving Rd SO16 42 D2
Irwell Cl SO53 20 C2
Isis Cl SO16 42 C4
Itchen Bri SO14 5 J5
Itchen Av SO50 23 E6
Itchen Vw SO18 31 G6
Itchenside Cl SO18 31 G6
Itchin Cl SO40 40 C5
Ivanhoe Rd SO15 43 H2
Ivor Cl SO45 68 D6
Ivy Cl SO40 41 E2
Ivy Dene SO19 60 C2
Ivy La SO30 46 A2
Ivy Rd SO17 44 D4

Jack Cl SO13 20 A1
Jackdaw Rise SO50 21 E6
Jackie Wigg Gdns
  SO40 41 G5
Jackmans Cl SO19 59 E3
Jacob Cl SO51 17 G1
Jacob Gutter La SO40 55 F1
Jacobs Walk SO40 55 F1
James Ct SO51 17 H1
James St SO14 5 F3
Jameson Rd SO19 59 G3
Janaway Gdns SO17 45 E4
Janes Cl SO45 70 D4
Janson Rd SO15 43 G5
Jarvis Flds SO31 61 G6
Jasmine Rd SO30 47 G4
Jeffries Cl SO16 28 B4
Jenkyns Cl SO30 48 C5
Jenner Way SO51 10 A6
Jennings Rd SO40 41 G4
Jermyns La SO51 10 A2
Jerome Ct SO19 46 B6
Jerretts La SO16 28 B6
Jersey Cl SO16 42 B1
Jervis Court La SO32 37 E2
Jessamine Rd SO16 43 E2
Jessica Cres SO40 40 B3
Jessie Ter SO14 5 E5
Jessop Cl SO45 67 F1
Jessop Walk SO45 67 E1
Jex Blake Cl SO16 29 F6
Jinny La SO51 9 E1
Jockey La SO50 22 C3
Joe Bigwood Cl SO16 28 B5
John Bunyan Cl PO15 63 E6
John St SO14 5 E5
Johns Rd SO19 59 E4
Johnson St SO14 5 E3
Jonas Nichols Sq SO14 5 H2
Jones La SO45 67 F2
Josian Walk SO14 5 F2
Jubilee Cl SO50 21 G6
Jubilee Ct SO30 61 F1
Jubilee Gdns SO18 45 H5
Jubilee Rd SO51 9 F6
Julian Cl SO16 30 A3
Julian Rd SO19 60 A3
Julius Cl SO53 21 G1
Junction Rd SO40 41 G5
Juniper Cl SO52 18 D3
Juniper Rd SO18 45 G5
Jupiter Cl SO16 28 C6
Jurd Way SO31 61 E5
Jurds Lake Way SO19 59 E5
Justinian Cl SO53 21 G1

Kanes Hill SO19 46 D5
Kathleen Rd SO19 59 H3
Kathryn Cl SO40 40 B3
Katie Johnson Gdns

SO15 44 A4
Katrine Cres SO53 12 B6
Kayleigh Cl SO40 40 D6
Keats Cl PO15 63 E5
Keats Rd SO18 46 B5
Keble Cl SO53 20 D3
Keble Rd SO53 20 D3
Keepers Cl SO53 20 D2
Kelburn Cl SO53 20 D1
Kellett Rd SO15 43 H3
Kelmscott Gdns SO53 12 C5
Kelston Cl SO15 43 E5
Kelvin Cl SO45 67 F3
Kelvin Gro SO31 64 C2
Kelvin Rd SO50 21 G6
Kemps Quay
  Ind Est SO18 45 E5
Kendal Av SO16 42 B3
Kendal Cl SO53 13 F6
Kendal Cl SO16 42 B3
Kenilworth Dr SO50 21 H2
Kenilworth Gdns SO30 46 D3
Kenilworth Rd SO15 44 A6
Kenmore Cl SO40 55 E1
Kennedy Rd SO16 42 D1
Kennet Cl SO18 46 A1
Kennett Cl SO51 10 A6
Kennett Rd SO51 10 A6
Kennington La SO40 52 D2
Kensington Cl SO50 22 C3
Kensington Flds SO45 66 D4
Kenson Gdns SO19 59 H2
Kent Gdns SO40 41 E6
Kent Rd,
  Eastleigh SO53 21 E4
Kent Rd,
  Southampton SO17 44 D3
Kent St SO14 5 G1
Kentish Rd SO15 43 F5
Kenwyn Cl SO18 46 A2
Kern Cl SO16 42 D1
Kerry Cl SO53 20 D1
Kersley Gdns SO19 59 H2
Kestevan Way SO18 46 A3
Kestrel Cl,
  Bishops Waltham
  SO32 36 A1
Kestrel Cl,
  Botley SO32 48 B3
Kestrel Cl,
  Marchwood SO40 56 C5
Kestrel Cl,
  Southampton SO16 29 E4
Kestrel Rd SO50 21 F6
Keswick Rd SO19 59 E3
Kevlyn Cres SO31 60 D5
Kew La SO31 61 F6
Kewlake La SO40 38 A5
Keynsham Rd SO19 46 A6
Khartoum Rd SO17 44 B2
Kielder Cl SO53 12 B6
Kilford Cl SO30 48 C5
Killarney Cl SO19 60 D3
Kiln Cl SO45 67 E4
Kiln Grn SO21 15 E5
Kiln La SO21 14 A3
Kilnyard Cl SO40 40 D3
Kimberley Cl SO30 23 H6
Kimbridge Cl SO16 28 C5
Kineton Rd SO15 43 H3
King Edward Av SO16 43 E4
King Georges Av SO15 42 D5
King St SO14 5 E5
Kingfisher Cl SO53 65 G4
Kingfisher Rd SO50 21 F6
Kingfisher Way,
  Romsey SO51 9 F5
Kingfisher Way,
  Southampton SO40 56 C5
Kings Av SO31 65 E5
Kings Cl,
  Eastleigh SO53 21 E1
Kings Cl,
  Winchester SO21 7 F4
Kings Copse Av SO30 48 A6
Kings Copse Rd,
  Blackfield SO45 70 B4
Kings Copse Rd,
  Hedge End SO30 61 H1
Kings Park Rd SO15 5 E1
Kings Rd SO53 21 E1
Kings Ride SO45 70 C5
Kings Way SO32 25 G3
Kingsbridge La SO14 4 C2
Kingsbury Rd SO14 44 C5
Kingsclere Av SO19 59 G5
Kingsclere Cl SO19 59 G5
Kingsdown Way SO18 45 H2
Kingsfield SO31 61 F5
Kingsfield Gdns SO31 61 F5
Kingsfold Av SO18 45 G1
Kingsland Ct SO14 5 E3
Kingsland Sq SO14 5 F3
Kingsley Gdns SO40 40 C5
Kingsley Rd SO15 43 F5
Kingston SO31 64 C1
Kingston Rd SO15 43 G6

Kingsway,
  Eastleigh SO53 13 E6
Kingsway,
  Southampton SO14 5 E2
Kingsway Cl SO53 13 G5
Kingsway Gdns SO53 13 F5
Kingswood SO50 56 D5
Kinross Rd SO40 41 F5
Kinsbourne Cl SO19 46 D6
Kinsbourne Rise SO19 46 D6
Kinsbourne Way SO19 46 D6
Kinver Cl SO51 9 H4
Kipling Cl PO15 63 E5
Kipling Ct SO19 59 G5
Kipling Rd SO50 21 G4
Kirk Gdns SO40 55 G1
Kitchener Rd SO17 44 D1
Kitnocks Hill SO32 49 G4
Knapp La SO51 11 G2
Knatchbull Cl SO51 17 G1
Knellers La SO40 54 D1
Knighton Rd SO19 59 G3
Knightsbridge Grange
  SO45 67 F4
Knightswood Vw
  SO53 20 D2
Knightwood Cl SO40 54 C4
Knightwood Glade
  SO53 12 B6
Knightwood Rd,
  Eastleigh SO53 12 B6
Knightwood Rd,
  Southampton SO45 67 G4
Knowle Hill SO50 22 A1
Knowle La SO50 24 B5
Knowles Cl SO16 28 B5
Knyght Cl SO51 17 G1
Kootenay Av SO18 46 C5
Kytes La SO32 34 D5

Laburnum Cl SO52 19 E3
Laburnum Cres SO45 68 C3
Laburnum Gro SO50 21 H4
Laburnum Rd,
  Hedge End SO30 48 A6
Laburnum Rd,
  Southampton SO16 30 D5
Lackford Av SO40 41 F6
Lackford Way SO40 41 F6
Lacon Cl SO18 45 F3
Ladycross Rd SO45 67 F5
Ladywood SO50 21 G2
Lake Farm Cl SO40 47 H4
Lake Rd,
  Curdridge SO32 49 H4
Lake Rd,
  Eastleigh SO53 13 F5
Lake Rd,
  Southampton SO19 59 E4
Lakeland Gdns SO40 56 C5
Lakelands Dr SO15 43 H6
Lakeside Av SO16 28 C4
Lakewood Cl SO53 13 F5
Lakewood Rd,
  Eastleigh SO53 13 F5
Lakewood Rd,
  Southampton SO40 54 C2
Lamberhurst Cl SO19 59 H6
Lambourn Sq SO53 20 C2
Lambourne Cl SO45 67 E5
Lambourne Rd SO18 45 H1
Lammas Rd SO45 67 E5
Lancaster Cl SO31 61 F5
Lancaster Rd SO16 42 D1
Lances Hill SO18 45 G5
Landguard Rd SO15 43 H6
Lands End Rd SO31 65 H1
Landseer Rd SO19 60 B2
Lanehays Rd SO45 67 E3
Lanesbridge Cl SO40 53 H4
Langbar Cl SO19 45 F6
Langdale Cl SO16 42 D4
Langdown Firs SO45 67 F4
Langdown Lawn SO45 67 F4
Langdown Lawn Cl
  SO45 67 F4
Langdown Rd SO45 67 F3
Langham Cl SO52 18 D4
Langhorn Rd SO16 31 E6
Langley Lodge Gdns
  SO45 70 D5
Langley Rd SO15 43 F6
Langrish Rd SO16 29 F6
Langton Rd SO32 36 B2
Lansdowne Cl SO51 9 E5
Lansdowne Gdns SO15 9 E5
Lansdowne Rd SO15 43 E4
Langbury Dr SO40 40 C1
Larch Av SO45 68 D5
Larch Cl SO30 43 E1
Larch Rd SO16 43 E1
Larch Way SO31 61 F6
Larchwood Rd SO40 40 C5
Larkspur Chase SO19 59 H6
Larkspur Cl SO32 37 G5
Larkspur Dr,
  Eastleigh SO53 20 A1

Larkspur Gdns,
  Hedge End SO30 47 H6
Larkspur Gdns,
  Holbury SO45 68 C6
Latchmore Dr SO45 66 C3
Latelie Cl SO31 64 C3
Latham Cl SO50 23 G5
Latham Ct SO15 43 F4
Latham Rd,
  Eastleigh SO50 23 F6
Latham Rd,
  Romsey SO51 9 G6
Latimer St,
  Romsey SO51 9 E6
Latimer St,
  Southampton SO14 5 E5
Launcelyn Cl SO52 18 D4
Launceston Dr SO50 21 G2
Laundry Rd SO16 43 E1
Laura Cl SO40 40 B3
Laurel Cl, Hythe SO45 67 E3
Laurel Cl,
  Southampton SO19 59 E3
Lauren Way SO40 40 B2
Laurence Mews SO51 9 F5
Lauriston Dr SO53 12 C5
Lavender Cl SO19 59 G1
Laverstoke Cl SO16 28 C4
Lavington Gdns SO52 18 D4
Lawford Way SO40 41 E4
Lawn Rd,
  Eastleigh SO50 22 A3
Lawn Rd,
  Southampton SO17 44 C4
Lawnside Rd SO15 43 E4
Lawnswood SO50 33 H1
Lawrence Gro SO19 59 G4
Lawson Cl SO31 62 A6
Laxton Cl SO19 59 H4
Leacock Cl SO32 37 G5
Leander Cl SO50 21 H2
Leaside Way SO16 30 D5
Leatherhead Gdns
  SO30 47 H2
Lebanon Rd SO15 42 A4
Leckford Cl SO18 46 B3
Lee Church La SO51 27 F1
Lee Dro SO51 17 H6
Lee La, Romsey SO51 17 G3
Lee La,
  Southampton SO16 27 G4
Legion Cl SO16 30 D6
Leicester Rd SO15 43 H2
Leigh Rd,
  Chandler's Ford SO53 20 D4
Leigh Rd,
  Eastleigh SO50 21 F4
Leigh Rd,
  Southampton SO15 43 F4
Leighton Av SO15 43 F4
Leighton Rd SO19 59 G3
Lemon Rd SO15 43 F4
Lennox Cl,
  Eastleigh SO53 13 F6
Lennox Cl,
  Southampton SO16 28 D4
Leopold Dr SO32 36 A2
Lepe Rd SO45 70 D5
Leroux Cl SO16 4 C1
Leven Cl SO53 12 B6
Lewes Cl SO50 21 H1
Lewin Cl SO21 15 E5
Lewins Walk SO31 61 E5
Lewis Cl SO45 66 C4
Lewis Silkin Way SO16 29 E5
Lewry Cl SO30 47 H5
Lexby Rd SO40 41 G6
Leybourne Av SO18 45 G4
Leyton Rd SO14 44 D5
Liberty Row SO31 65 G6
Library Rd SO40 41 G4
Lichen Way SO40 56 D4
Liddel Way SO53 20 C2
Lightning Cl SO45 71 E2
Lilac Rd SO16 30 C5
Lilley Cl SO40 54 C4
Lime Av SO19 59 H1
Lime Cl,
  Dibden Purlieu SO45 66 D5
Lime Cl,
  Southampton SO19 59 H1
Lime Cl,
  Winchester SO21 15 F5
Lime Gdns SO30 46 C1
Lime Kiln La SO45 68 C5
Lime St SO14 5 E4
Lime Walk,
  Botley SO30 48 B4
Lime Walk,
  Dibden Purlieu SO45 66 D5
Linacre Rd SO19 60 C1
Lincoln Cl SO51 9 H4
Lincoln Ct SO15 43 H2
Lincolns Rise SO50 14 A5
Linda Rd SO45 71 G1
Linden Cl SO32 51 E1

Linden Gdns SO30 47 H6
Linden Gro SO53 12 D5
Linden Rd,
  Romsey SO51 9 F6
Linden Rd,
  Southampton SO16 29 E6
Linden Walk SO50 18 D2
Lindsay Rd SO19 46 B6
Linford Cres SO16 43 G1
Linford Ct SO50 23 H6
Lingdale SO16 30 A3
Lingfield Gdns SO18 45 G1
Lingwood Cl SO16 30 A3
Lingwood Walk SO16 30 A3
Link Rd SO16 42 D1
Links View Way SO16 30 A3
Linnet Sq SO50 21 E6
Linwood Cl SO45 67 F5
Lionheart Way SO31 61 E5
Lipizzaner Flds PO15 62 D6
Lisbon Rd SO15 43 G6
Litchfield Cres SO18 45 G2
Litchfield Rd SO18 45 G3
Little Bull La SO32 50 D2
Little Kimble Walk
  SO30 47 G6
Little Lances Hill SO19 45 G5
Little Meads SO51 17 E1
Little Oak Rd SO16 30 A5
Little Park Cl SO30 47 G6
Little Quob La SO30 46 D1
Little Reynolds SO40 54 D1
Little Shore La SO32 36 C2
Littlefield Cres SO53 20 A2
Littlewood Gdns SO30 46 C3
Liverpool St SO14 44 B5
Livingstone Rd SO14 44 C4
Lloyd Av SO40 56 C5
Loane Rd SO19 59 G2
Lobelia Rd SO16 30 D5
Locke Rd SO30 47 H4
Lockerley Cres SO16 42 D2
Lockhams Rd SO32 49 G4
Locks Cotts SO45 66 C1
Locksley Rd SO50 21 F6
Lodge Dr SO45 67 F5
Lodge Rd SO14 44 B4
Lofting Cl SO50 22 C5
Logan Cl SO16 28 D4
Lomax Cl SO30 47 G3
London Rd SO15 4 D1
Long Beech Dr SO40 41 E6
Long Cl SO30 46 D2
Long La,
  Bursledon SO31 61 F6
Long La,
  Holbury SO45 68 C4
Long La,
  Marchwood SO40 56 B5
Long Lane Cl SO45 70 C1
Longbridge SO40 40 D1
Longbridge Ct SO40 40 D1
Longbridge Ind Est
  SO14 5 G5
Longclose Rd SO30 47 H5
Longcroft SO14 5 G3
Longfield Rd SO50 23 H6
Longleat Gdns SO16 29 F5
Longmead Av SO50 22 C3
Longmead Rd SO18 45 H2
Longmeadow Gdns
  SO45 67 F3
Longmore Av SO19 59 E6
Longmore Cres SO19 59 E6
Longridge Rd SO30 47 H6
Longstock Cl SO19 59 G6
Longstock Cres SO40 41 E5
Loperwood SO40 39 H5
Loperwood La SO40 26 A6
Lord Mountbatten Cl
  SO18 31 F6
Lords Hill Centre East
  SO16 28 D5
Lords Hill Centre West
  SO16 28 D5
Lords Hill District Centre
  SO16 28 C6
Lords Hill Way SO16 28 C6
Lordshill SO50 14 C6
Lordswood Cl SO16 29 G6
Lordswood Ct SO16 29 G5
Lordswood Gdns SO16 29 H6
Lordswood La SO16 29 G6
Lordswood Rd SO16 29 G6
Loreille Gdns SO16 28 C3
Lortemore Pl SO51 9 F6
Loughwood Cl SO50 21 H2
Lovage Gdns SO40 40 C5
Lovage Rd PO15 63 F6
Love La, Romsey SO51 17 F1
Love La,
  Winchester SO21 7 H4
Lower Alfred St SO14 44 C4
Lower Banister St
  SO15 44 B6
Lower Brownhill Rd

SO16 42 A2
Lower Canal Walk SO14 5 E6
Lower Chase Rd SO32 37 E6
Lower La SO32 36 C2
Lower Moors Rd SO21 15 E4
Lower Mortimer Rd SO19 59 F2
Lower Mullins La SO45 67 E3
Lower New Rd SO30 46 C2
Lower Northam Rd SO30 47 G5
Lower St Helens Rd SO30 61 G1
Lower Swanwick Rd SO31 62 A6
Lower Vicarage Rd SO19 59 E3
Lower William St SO14 45 E6
Lower York St SO14 45 E6
Lowford Hill SO31 61 E5
Lowry Gdns SO19 60 B4
Lucas Cl SO16 28 D5
Luccombe Pl SO15 43 H2
Luccombe Rd SO15 43 H1
Lucerne Gdns SO30 47 F5
Ludlow Rd SO19 59 F2
Ludwells La SO32 37 E5
Lukes Cl SO31 65 G6
Lukin Dr SO16 28 A4
Lulworth Bsns Pk SO40 41 E1
Lulworth Cl, Eastleigh SO53 20 C5
Lulworth Cl, Southampton SO16 42 C2
Lulworth Grn SO16 42 C1
Lumsden Av SO15 43 G5
Lundy Cl SO16 28 C5
Lunedale Rd SO45 66 D6
Lupin Rd SO16 30 D5
Luton Rd SO19 60 A1
Luxton Cl SO30 48 C4
Luzborough La SO51 17 H4
Lyburn Cl SO16 29 F6
Lydgate Cl SO19 60 C1
Lydgate Grn SO19 60 C2
Lydgate Rd SO19 60 C2
Lydiard Cl SO30 21 H2
Lydlynch Rd SO40 41 F5
Lyme Cl SO30 21 G3
Lymer La SO16 28 A3
Lymer Villas SO16 28 A4
Lynden Gate SO19 59 H3
Lyndhurst Rd, Lyndhurst SO43 54 A6
Lyndhurst Rd, Southampton SO40 52 B2
Lyndock Cl SO19 59 F4
Lyndock Pl SO19 59 F4
Lynn Cl SO18 45 H1
Lynton Ct SO40 41 E6
Lynton Rd SO30 47 G5
Lynx Cl SO50 23 E6
Lyon St SO14 44 B6
Lytham Rd SO18 45 H3
Lytton Rd SO45 67 G4

Macarthur Cres SO14 45 H4
Macnaghten Rd SO18 45 F5
Maddison St SO14 4 D4
Maddoxford La SO32 48 B2
Maddoxford Way SO32 48 B2
Maesfield Grn SO19 46 C6
Maffey Ct SO30 48 C5
Magazine La SO40 56 D3
Magnolia Cl SO45 66 C3
Magnolia Gro SO50 24 A5
Magnolia Rd SO19 59 G1
Magpie Dr SO40 40 D5
Magpie Gdns SO19 60 B2
Magpie La SO50 21 F6
Main Rd, Colden Common SO21 15 E3
Main Rd, Dibden SO45 66 C1
Main Rd, Holbury SO45 68 D4
Main Rd, Marchwood SO40 56 C5
Main Rd, Otterbourne SO21 14 A3
Main Rd, Totton SO40 55 E2
Mainstone SO51 16 D2
Mainstream Ct SO50 22 C5
Majestic Rd SO16 27 H6
Malcolm Cl SO53 13 F5
Malcolm Rd SO53 13 F5
Malcroft Mews SO40 57 E5
Maldon Cl SO14 22 C4
Maldon Rd SO19 59 F1
Malibres Rd SO53 13 G5
Malin Cl SO16 28 C5
Mallard Cl, Romsey SO51 9 G6
Mallard Cl,

Southampton SO32 36 A2
Mallard Gdns SO30 47 G2
Mallards Rd SO31 61 E6
Mallett Cl SO30 48 A2
Mallow Rd SO30 47 H6
Malmesbury Cl SO50 23 G5
Malmesbury Pl SO15 43 G5
Malmesbury Rd, Romsey SO51 9 F6
Malmesbury Rd, Southampton SO15 43 G5
Malory Cl SO19 46 B6
Malt La SO32 36 C2
Malthouse Cl SO51 9 E6
Malthouse Gdns SO40 56 D5
Malvern Cl SO32 36 C2
Malvern Dr SO45 66 D4
Malvern Gdns SO30 47 H2
Malvern Rd SO16 43 G1
Malvern Ter SO16 43 G1
Malwood Av SO16 43 G1
Malwood Gdns SO40 40 C4
Malwood Rd SO45 67 E2
Malwood Rd West SO45 67 E3
Manaton Way SO30 47 F3
Manchester Rd SO31 64 A3
Manchester St SO14 4 D3
Mandela Way SO15 4 B1
Manley Rd SO31 61 E5
Manns Cl SO18 46 B2
Manor Cl, Bursledon SO31 60 D5
Manor Cl, Fareham PO17 72 D6
Manor Cl, Totton SO40 41 E6
Manor Cres SO31 61 E5
Manor Farm Cl SO50 22 C5
Manor Farm Grn SO21 15 E1
Manor Farm Gro SO50 22 C5
Manor Farm Rd SO18 45 G2
Manor House Av SO15 42 C5
Manor Rd, Chilworth SO16 19 H6
Manor Rd, Dibden SO45 66 A2
Manor Rd, Durley SO32 35 F2
Manor Rd, Eastleigh SO50 22 D6
Manor Rd, Holbury SO45 68 D6
Manor Rd, Winchester SO21 7 E6
Manor Rd North SO19 59 F2
Manor Road South SO19 59 F3
Manor Ter SO31 60 D5
Mansbridge Cotts SO18 31 G6
Mansbridge Rd, Eastleigh SO50 31 H1
Mansbridge Rd, Southampton SO18 46 A1
Mansbridge Rd, Swaythling SO18 31 F5
Mansel Ct SO16 42 C2
Mansel Rd East SO16 42 C2
Mansel Rd West SO16 42 B1
Mansell Cl SO45 66 D5
Mansergh Walk SO40 40 B4
Mansion Rd SO15 43 G6
Manston Cres SO16 28 D6
Maple Cl SO51 18 A1
Maple Gdns SO40 40 C5
Maple Rd, Hythe SO45 68 C2
Maple Rd, Southampton SO15 43 F6
Maple Sq SO50 21 F6
Mapleleaf Gdns SO50 21 F6
Mapleton Rd SO30 47 H6
Maplewood Cl SO40 40 C5
Maplin Rd SO16 42 B2
Marathon Pl SO50 21 E3
Marchwood By-Pass SO40 41 F6
Marchwood Ind Pk SO40 57 E3
Marchwood Rd, Marchwood SO40 56 A2
Marchwood Rd, Southampton SO15 43 F6
Marchwood Ter SO40 56 D4
Marcus Cl SO50 23 F6
Mardale Rd SO16 42 B4
Mardale Walk SO16 42 B4
Mardon Cl SO18 31 F5
Margam Av SO19 59 G1
Marie Rd SO19 60 B2
Marina Dr SO31 65 G5
Marine Par SO14 5 G4
Mariners Cl SO31 65 G4
Mariners Mews SO45 67 G3
Maritime Av SO40 56 D3
Maritime Cl SO45 5 F6
Maritime Way SO14 5 E6
Marjoram Way PO15 63 F6

Mark Cl SO15 43 E5
Market Pl, Romsey SO51 17 E1
Market Pl, Southampton SO14 4 D5
Market St SO50 21 H6
Marlbor Ugh Gdns SO30 47 G1
Winchester Ct, Eastleigh SO53 20 B3
Winchester Ct, Southampton SO45 67 E4
Winchester Rd, Eastleigh SO53 13 G4
Winchester Rd, Southampton SO15 43 F4
Marlhill Cl SO18 45 H5
Marlow Rd SO32 36 A1
Marlowe Ct SO19 59 G5
Marls Rd SO30 48 A5
Marne Rd SO18 45 H5
Marrianne Cl SO15 42 D5
Marsh Gdns SO30 47 G1
Marsh La, Fawley SO45 71 F1
Marsh La, Southampton SO14 5 F4
Marsh Par SO45 67 F2
Marshall Dr SO30 47 E3
Marshfield Cl SO40 56 B4
Marston Rd SO19 60 C1
Martin Cl SO32 37 G6
Martin St SO32 36 B2
Martindale Ter*, Windrush Rd SO16 42 C3
Martins Flds SO21 6 B3
Martley Gdns SO30 47 H1
Marvin Cl SO30 48 A5
Marvin Way, Botley SO30 48 A5
Marvin Way, Southampton SO18 46 B5
Marybridge Cl SO40 41 E6
Maryfield SO14 5 F4
Maryland Cl SO18 46 B5
Masefield Cl SO50 21 G4
Matheson Rd SO16 28 D4
Matley Gdns SO40 40 C5
Maunsell Way SO30 47 H3
Mauretania Rd SO16 27 H6
Maxwell Rd SO19 59 H3
May Cl SO45 70 C1
May Copse SO45 70 C1
May Cres SO45 70 C1
May Rd SO15 43 F5
Maybray King Way SO18 45 G5
Maybush Cl SO16 42 D2
Maybush Rd SO16 42 C2
Mayfair Ct SO30 48 C5
Mayfair Gdns SO15 44 A5
Mayfield Av SO40 41 G6
Mayfield Rd SO17 30 C6
Mayflower Cl SO53 20 C3
Mayflower Rd SO15 43 F4
Mayhill La SO32 37 H4
Mayles Cl PO17 72 C6
Mayles La PO17 72 C6
Maynard Rd SO40 41 F5
Maypole Villas SO50 13 H5
Maytree Cl SO50 24 A6
Maytree Rd, Eastleigh SO53 13 E4
Maytree Rd, Southampton SO18 45 H5
Mayvale Cl SO40 56 C5
Meacher Cl SO40 41 E4
Mead Cl SO15 9 H6
Mead Cres SO18 45 E1
Mead Rd SO53 20 D2
Meadbrook Gdns SO53 21 E2
Meadow Cl, North Baddesley SO52 19 E4
Meadow Cl, Totton SO40 55 F1
Meadow Cl, Waltham Chase SO32 36 D6
Meadow Cl, West End SO30 46 D1
Meadow Gdns SO30 36 D6
Meadow Gro SO53 20 D4
Meadow La SO31 65 G6
Meadow Way SO45 71 F1
Meadowcroft Cl SO21 14 B2
Meadowhead Rd SO16 30 A6
Meadowmead Av SO15 43 E5
Meadowside Cl SO18 31 F6
Meadowsweet Way SO50 33 H3
Mears Rd SO30 24 A6
Medina Cl SO53 21 F3
Medina Rd SO15 43 F3
Medlar Cl SO30 47 H5
Medlicott Way SO32 37 G5

Medwall Grn SO19 60 C1
Medway Dr SO53 12 B6
Megan Rd SO30 46 C2
Meggeson Av SO18 45 G1
Melbourne Gdns SO30 47 H6
Melbourne Rd SO30 47 H6
Melbourne St SO14 5 G4
Melchet Rd SO18 46 B4
Melick Cl SO40 56 D4
Melrose Cl SO45 43 H1
Melrose Rd SO15 43 H1
Melville Cl SO16 29 G4
Mendip Gdns SO45 66 D4
Mendip Rd SO16 42 D4
Menzies Cl SO31 28 D5
Meon Cl SO51 10 A6
Meon Cres SO31 21 E2
Meon Ct SO18 46 C4
Meon Gdns SO32 37 G4
Meon Rd SO51 10 A6
Mercer Way SO51 9 G5
Merchants Walk SO14 4 D5
Mercury Cl SO16 28 D6
Mercury Gdns SO31 65 G4
Merdon Av SO53 13 E6
Merdon Cl SO53 13 E6
Meredith Gdns SO40 40 D6
Merlin Cl SO32 36 B2
Merlin Gdns SO30 47 G4
Merlins Way SO53 20 A1
Mermaid Way SO14 5 F6
Merrick Way SO53 12 B6
Merridale Rd SO19 59 F2
Merrieleas Cl SO53 20 D1
Merrieleas Dr SO53 20 D1
Merriemeade Cl SO45 67 E6
Merriemeade Par SO45 67 E6
Merrivale Cl SO45 67 E3
Merry Gdns SO52 19 E3
Merryoak Grn SO19 59 G1
Merryoak Rd SO19 59 G1
Mersea Gdns SO19 59 H2
Mersham Gdns SO18 45 H5
Merton Rd SO17 44 C1
Methuen St SO14 44 B5
Metuchen Way SO30 61 G2
Mews Ct SO21 14 A3
Meynell Cl SO50 21 G4
Michaels Way, Eastleigh SO50 24 A6
Michaels Way, Southampton SO45 67 E2
Michelmersh Cl SO16 28 C4
Michigan Way SO40 40 B3
Midanbury Cres SO18 45 G3
Midanbury La SO18 45 F5
Midanbury Walk SO18 45 G3
Middle Rd, North Baddesley SO52 19 E3
Middle Rd, Southampton SO19 59 H3
Middle St, Bishops Waltham SO32 36 C2
Middle St, Southampton SO14 44 B5
Middlebridge St SO51 17 E1
Middlebrook SO32 36 C2
Middleton Cl SO18 45 H2
Midlands Est SO30 46 B2
Midway SO45 67 E4
Milbury Cres SO18 45 H5
Mile Ride SO52 19 G2
Milford Dr SO53 21 F2
Milkwood Ct SO40 40 C5
Mill Cl SO16 28 B4
Mill Ct SO50 23 H6
Mill Hill SO30 48 D5
Mill La, Droxford SO32 35 H6
Mill La, Nursling SO16 27 E6
Mill La, Romsey SO51 9 F6
Mill La, Wickham PO17 72 D4
Mill Rd, Southampton SO15 42 D5
Mill Rd, Totton SO40 41 G5
Mill St SO50 22 A4
Mill Way SO40 55 E1
Millais Rd SO19 59 F3
Millbank St SO14 5 H1
Millbridge Gdns SO50 60 A2
Millbrook Cl SO53 20 D2
Millbrook Flyover SO15 42 C5
Millbrook Point Rd SO15 43 E6
Millbrook Rd East SO15 4 A1
Millbrook Rd West SO15 42 C5
Millbrook Trading Est SO15 42 C5
Millers Pond Gdns SO19 59 G3
Millers Way SO45 67 E5
Milliken Cl SO45 71 E2
Millstream Rise SO51 8 D6
Millvina Cl SO40 53 H5

Milne Cl SO45 66 C4
Milner Ct SO15 43 F3
Milton Rd, Eastleigh SO50 22 A2
Milton Rd, Southampton SO15 44 A6
Milverton Cl SO40 41 G6
Milverton Rd SO40 41 G6
Mimosa Dr SO30 24 A5
Mincingfield La SO32 35 F6
Mincingfield Ter SO32 35 F5
Minstead Av SO18 46 B4
Minstead Rd SO43 52 A6
Mintern Cl SO50 22 C3
Mislingford Rd SO32 37 H6
Missenden Acres SO30 24 A6
Misslebrook La SO52 19 G4
Mitchell Cl SO19 59 E3
Mitchell Dr SO50 23 G5
Mitchell Point SO31 72 B1
Mitchell Rd SO50 22 A5
Mitchell Way SO18 31 G3
Mitchells Cl SO51 9 F6
Mitre Copse SO50 23 E5
Moat Cl SO45 70 A1
Moat Hill SO18 45 G1
Mon Cres SO18 46 B5
Monarch Way SO30 46 D2
Monarchs Way SO21 7 G5
Monastery Rd SO18 45 H2
Monks Brook Ind Pk SO53 20 C2
Monks Path SO18 31 F6
Monks Pl SO40 41 E6
Monks Rd SO31 64 B2
Monks Walk SO45 68 A2
Monks Way, Eastleigh SO50 31 F1
Monks Way, Southampton SO18 31 F5
Monks Wood Cl SO16 30 C4
Monksbrook Cl SO50 31 F1
Monkton La SO40 40 D6
Monmouth Cl SO53 20 D2
Monmouth Gdns SO40 54 D1
Monnow Gdns SO18 46 A2
Montague Av SO19 60 C3
Montague Cl SO19 60 C3
Montague Rd SO50 22 C5
Montfort Cl SO51 18 A1
Montfort Heights SO51 18 A1
Montfort Rd SO51 18 A2
Montgomery Av SO40 41 E4
Montgomery Rd SO18 45 H4
Montgomery Way SO53 20 C5
Montrose Cl SO30 48 A6
Moon Cl SO40 56 C5
Mooncross Av SO40 55 F1
Moore Cres SO31 64 C1
Moorgreen Rd SO30 46 D2
Moorhead Ct SO14 5 G6
Moorhill Gdns SO18 46 C3
Moorhill Rd SO30 46 C3
Moorland Cl SO45 66 C4
Moorlands Cres SO18 45 H4
Moorlands Rd SO32 37 F3
Moors Cl SO21 14 D4
Mopley SO45 71 E5
Mopley Cl SO45 70 D5
Mordaunt Rd SO14 44 B5
Morgan Le Fay Dr SO52/53 12 A6
Morgan Rd SO30 47 G6
Morland Rd SO15 43 G2
Morley Cl SO19 45 G6
Morley Dr SO32 36 B2
Morpeth Av SO40 41 F4
Morris Cl SO45 66 C3
Morris Rd SO15 4 C1
Morse Ct SO31 64 A2
Mortimer Cl, Netley SO31 64 B2
Mortimer Cl, Totton SO40 40 D3
Mortimer Rd, Botley SO30 48 C5
Mortimer Rd, Southampton SO19 59 F2
Mortimer Way SO52 18 D4
Mortimers Dr SO50 23 H6
Mortimers La, Fair Oak SO50 23 H6
Mortimers La, Upham SO32 25 E4
Mosaic Cl SO19 60 D2
Mosedale Walk SO16 42 B4
Moss Dr SO40 56 B5
Mossleigh Av SO18 28 D4
Mottisfont Cl SO15 44 A6
Mottisfont Rd SO50 21 H4
Mottistone Cl SO53 21 F3
Mount House Cl SO45 67 F1
Mount Pleasant

Ind Est SO14 44 C5
Mount Pleasant Rd SO14 44 C5
Mount Pleasant*, Broadwater Rd SO51 17 E1
Mount Temple SO51 17 G1
Mount Vw SO50 22 A4
Mountain Ash Cl SO18 46 B5
Mountbatten Av SO51 9 F6
Mountbatten Bsns Centre SO15 4 A2
Mountbatten Rd, Eastleigh SO50 21 H2
Mountbatten Rd, Southampton SO40 41 E4
Mountbatten Retail Pk SO14 4 A2
Mountbatten Way SO15 4 A2
Mountfield SO45 66 D2
Mousehole La, Hythe SO45 67 F3
Mousehole La, Southampton SO18 45 G4
Mowbray Rd SO19 60 A2
Mulberry Rd SO40 56 D5
Mulberry Walk SO15 43 G4
Mullen Cl SO19 59 F2
Munro Cres SO15 42 D5
Murray Cl SO19 46 D6
Mussett Cl SO40 41 E4
Myers Cl SO32 37 G5
Myrtle Av SO40 40 D6
Myrtle Rd SO16 29 E6
Myvern Cl SO45 70 C2

Napier Rd SO19 60 C1
Narrow La SO51 17 E1
Nash Cl SO45 66 D5
Nash Rd SO45 66 C5
Navigators Way SO30 47 G3
Neath Way SO53 20 B2
Neilson Cl SO53 12 D6
Nelson Bsns Pk SO30 47 G3
Nelson Cl, Romsey SO51 9 G6
Nelson Cl, Southampton SO45 70 B1
Nelson Ct SO45 67 G5
Nelson Gate SO15 4 B2
Nelson Gdns SO30 47 G1
Nelson Hill SO15 4 B2
Nelson Rd, Eastleigh SO50 22 C4
Nelson Rd, Southampton SO15 43 F6
Neptune Ct SO16 28 D6
Neptune Way SO14 5 F6
Nerquis Cl SO51 9 H6
Netherhill La SO32 48 D2
Netley Cl SO53 20 C4
Netley Firs Rd SO19 61 E2
Netley Firs Rd SO30 47 E6
Netley Hill SO19 61 E2
Netley Lodge Cl SO31 64 C3
Nettlestone SO31 64 C1
Neva Rd SO18 45 G3
Neville Cl SO51 9 F5
New Cotts SO16 42 A1
New Forest Enterprise Centre SO40 55 E1
New Inn La SO40 53 E3
New Inn Rd SO40 53 E3
New Rd, Ashurst SO40 54 C3
New Rd, Blackfield SO45 70 D3
New Rd, Eastleigh SO50 23 F6
New Rd, Hardley SO45 68 D2
New Rd, Hythe SO45 67 F2
New Rd, Netley SO31 64 A2
New Rd, Romsey SO51 9 G5
New Rd, Southampton SO14 4 D2
New Rd, Swanick SO31 62 B6
New Rd, Swanmore SO32 37 F6
New Rd, Winchester SO21 15 E4
Newbridge Cl SO52 64 C2
Newbridge Rd SO40 38 C4
Newbury Cl SO50 23 G6
Newbury Rd SO15 43 F3
Newcliffe Gdns SO30 47 F6
Newcombe Rd SO15 4 C1
Newlands Av SO15 43 G5
Newlands Cl, Eastleigh SO50 23 A2
Newlands Cl, Southampton SO45 70 D4
Newlands Copse SO45 70 D3
Newlands Rd SO45 70 D2
Newlyn Walk SO51 9 G5
Newman St SO16 43 F3
Newmans Copse Rd SO40 55 G2
Newmans Hill PO17 51 H4

Newmarket Cl SO50 34 A3
Newport Cl SO53 20 B4
Newton La SO51 17 E1
Newton Rd, Southampton SO18 45 F3
Newton Rd, Winchester SO21 7 F4
Newtown Rd, Eastleigh SO50 21 H4
Newtown Rd, Southampton SO19 59 H4
Nichol Rd SO53 13 E4
Nicholas Rd SO45 70 D5
Nichols Rd SO14 5 F2
Nicholson Walk SO16 28 B4
Nickleby Gdns SO40 40 C5
Nickson Cl SO53 12 D6
Nightingale Av SO16 21 E6
Nightingale Cl, Romsey SO51 17 H1
Nightingale Cl, Southampton SO31 61 E6
Nightingale Cres SO32 51 F4
Nightingale Dr SO40 40 C4
Nightingale Gro SO15 43 G5
Nightingale Mews SO31 64 C3
Nightingale Rd SO15 43 G5
Nightingale Walk SO31 64 C3
Nile Rd SO17 44 B2
Ninian Cl SO50 33 G1
Ninth St SO45 69 E6
Noads Cl SO45 67 E5
Noads Way SO45 66 D5
Noble Rd SO30 48 A6
Nobs Crook SO21 15 E6
Nomad Cl SO18 46 A3
Norbury Cl SO53 20 D1
Norbury Gdns SO31 65 E6
Norcliffe Rd SO17 44 B3
Norcroft Ct SO16 43 G2
Nordik Gdns SO30 61 G1
Norfolk Ct*, Falkland Rd SO53 20 D6
Norfolk Rd SO15 43 G4
Norham Av SO16 43 G2
Norham Cl SO16 43 G2
Norlands Dr SO21 14 B2
Norman Gdns SO30 61 F1
Norman Rd, Blackfield SO45 70 D4
Norman Rd, Southampton SO15 57 G1
Normandy Cl SO16 28 B3
Normandy Ct PO17 72 D5
Normandy Way SO40 56 C3
Norris Cl SO51 10 A4
Norris Hill SO18 45 F3
North Cl SO51 10 A4
North East Cl SO19 60 A1
North East Rd SO19 59 H2
North End Cl SO53 20 D3
North Front SO14 5 E2
North Millers Dale SO53 12 C5
North Rd, Dibden Purlieu SO45 66 D4
North Rd, Southampton SO17 44 D3
Northam Bri SO14 44 D5
Northam Rd SO14 5 F2
Northam St SO14 5 F2
Northampton La SO45 70 D4
Northbourne Cl SO45 67 F6
Northbrook Ind Est SO16 43 G1
Northbrook Rd SO14 5 G1
Northcote Rd SO17 44 D2
Northdene Rd SO53 20 D3
Northern Anchorage SO19 5 H5
Northerwood Cl SO52 18 D3
Northfield Cl SO32 36 A1
Northfield Rd SO18 45 G1
Northfields SO21 7 F4
Northfields Farm La PO17 51 G6
Northlands Cl SO40 41 E4
Northlands Gdns SO15 44 A5
Northlands Rd, Eastleigh SO50 21 H4
Northlands Rd, Romsey SO51 18 A1
Northlands Rd, Southampton SO15 44 A5
Northlands Rd, Totton SO40 41 E4
Northleigh Cnr SO18 31 F5
Northolt Gdns SO16 29 E5
Northumberland Rd SO14 5 F2
Northwood Cl SO16 30 C4
Norton Cl SO19 59 F3
Norton Welch Cl SO52 19 E4
Norwich Rd SO18 45 G2
Noyce Dr SO50 23 H6
Nursery Gdns,

Eastleigh SO53 20 D5
Nursery Gdns, Romsey SO51 17 G1
Nursery Gdns, Southampton SO19 46 A5
Nursery Gro SO30 61 G1
Nursery Rd SO18 45 E2
Nurses Path SO21 7 F6
Nursling Ind Est SO16 27 H6
Nursling St SO16 28 A5
Nutbeem Rd SO50 21 H6
Nutburn Rd SO52 19 E3
Nutfield Ct SO16 42 C1
Nutfield Rd SO16 28 B4
Nutsey Av SO40 41 E2
Nutsey Cl SO40 41 E1
Nutsey La SO40 41 E2
Nutshalling Av SO16 28 B4
Nutshalling Cl SO40 40 C2
Nutwood Way SO40 41 E1

Oak Cl, Dibden Purlieu SO45 66 D6
Oak Cl, Southampton SO15 42 A4
Oak Cl, Upham SO32 25 H2
Oak Coppice Cl SO50 23 F5
Oak Dr SO50 23 H6
Oak Green Way SO18 45 H3
Oak Rd, Bishops Waltham SO32 36 D2
Oak Rd, Bursledon SO31 61 E6
Oak Rd, Dibden Purlieu SO45 66 D6
Oak Rd, Southampton SO19 59 F4
Oak Tree Cl SO21 15 E5
Oak Tree Way SO50 21 H3
Oak Vale SO30 46 A1
Oak Walk SO50 23 H6
Oakbank Rd, Eastleigh SO50 22 B4
Oakbank Rd, Southampton SO19 59 E3
Oakdene SO40 40 C5
Oakenbrow SO45 66 C4
Oakfield Rd, Bartley SO40 53 E2
Oakfield Rd, Totton SO40 41 F4
Oakfields SO50 13 H6
Oakgrove Gdns SO50 22 C6
Oakgrove Rd SO50 22 D6
Oakhill SO31 61 F5
Oakhill Cl, Eastleigh SO53 21 F2
Oakhill Cl, Southampton SO31 61 F5
Oakhill Ter SO31 61 F5
Oakhurst Cl SO31 64 C2
Oakhurst Rd SO17 44 B1
Oakhurst Way SO31 64 C2
Oakland Dr SO40 56 D5
Oaklands Av SO40 41 F4
Oaklands Cl, Dibden Purlieu SO45 66 C5
Oaklands Way, Southampton SO16 30 B6
Oakleaf Cl SO40 56 D6
Oakleigh Cres SO40 41 E6
Oakleigh Gdns SO51 17 G1
Oakley Cl SO45 68 D6
Oakley John Walk SO19 45 G6
Oakley Rd SO16 42 C3
Oakmount Av, Eastleigh SO53 21 E3
Oakmount Av, Southampton SO17 44 B2
Oakmount Av, Totton SO40 41 F4
Oakmount Rd SO53 21 F4
Oakridge Rd SO15 42 A4
Oaktree Gdns SO30 47 G6
Oaktree Rd SO18 45 F7
Oakwood Av SO21 14 B2
Oakwood Cl, Eastleigh SO53 13 E5
Oakwood Cl, Romsey SO51 10 A4
Oakwood Cl, Winchester SO21 14 B2
Oakwood Ct SO30 46 D1
Oakwood Dr SO16 29 F4
Oakwood Rd SO53 13 E6
Oakwood Way SO31 65 G5
Oatfield Gdns SO40 40 D3
Oatlands SO51 9 F5
Oatlands Cl SO32 48 B2
Oatlands Rd SO32 48 B2
Obelisk Rd SO19 59 E4
Ocean Rd SO14 58 C5
Ocean Way SO14 5 F6
Ocknell Gro SO45 66 C3

Oconnell Rd SO50 21 F6
Octavia Gdns SO53 21 G1
Octavia Rd SO18 31 F6
Odiham Cl, Eastleigh SO53 20 C5
Odiham Cl, Southampton SO16 28 D6
Ogle Rd SO14 4 D3
Okement Cl SO18 46 A2
Old Bridge Cl SO31 61 G5
Old Bridge House Rd SO31 61 G5
Old Cracknore Cl SO40 56 D4
Old Farm Dr SO18 45 G1
Old Ivy La SO18 46 A2
Old Lyndhurst Rd SO40 52 C1
Old Magazine Cl SO40 56 D4
Old Mill Way SO16 42 D2
Old Parsonage Ct SO21 14 A2
Old Priory Cl SO31 72 C2
Old Rd, Romsey SO51 9 G5
Old Rd, Southampton SO14 5 F6
Old Rectory La SO21 7 E5
Old Redbridge Rd SO15 42 A4
Old Romsey Rd SO40 52 B1
Old Salisbury La SO51 8 A4
Old School Cl, Holbury SO45 68 D4
Old School Cl, Netley SO31 64 D1
Old School Gdns SO30 46 D2
Old Shamblehurst La SO30 47 H2
Old Spring La SO32 37 G5
Old Swanwick La SO31 61 H6
Oldbarn Cl SO40 40 C2
Oldbury Ct SO16 42 B1
Oldenburg PO15 62 D5
Oleander Dr SO40 40 B3
Olive Rd SO16 29 E6
Oliver Rd SO18 45 E1
Olivers Cl SO40 40 B5
Olympic Way SO50 23 F5
Omdurman Rd SO17 44 B2
Omega Bsns Pk SO53 20 D2
Onibury Cl SO18 45 H3
Onibury Rd SO18 45 H3
Onslow Rd SO14 44 C6
Orchard Av SO50 23 E6
Orchard Cl, Fawley SO45 71 F1
Orchard Cl, North Baddesley SO52 18 D2
Orchard Cl, Totton SO40 55 F1
Orchard Cl, Winchester SO21 15 E4
Orchard Ct SO30 48 A5
Orchard La, Romsey SO51 9 F6
Orchard La, Southampton SO14 5 E5
Orchard Pl SO14 5 E6
Orchard Rd SO50 23 G5
Orchard Way SO45 67 E4
Orchardlea SO32 37 H6
Orchards Way, Southampton SO17 44 B2
Orchards Way, West End SO30 46 B3
Ordnance Rd SO15 44 B6
Ordnance Way SO40 56 D3
Oregon Cl SO19 59 H2
Oriana Way SO16 27 H5
Oriental Ter SO14 4 D5
Orion Cl SO16 28 C6
Orion Ind Centre SO18 31 F4
Orkney Cl SO16 28 C5
Ormesby Dr SO53 12 C5
Ormond Cl SO50 23 F5
Orpen Rd SO19 60 B3
Orwell Cl SO15 42 C3
Osborne Cl SO31 64 D3
Osborne Dr SO53 21 F3
Osborne Gdns, Eastleigh SO50 23 A6
Osborne Gdns, Southampton SO17 44 D2
Osborne Rd SO40 41 G5
Osborne Rd North SO17 44 D3
Osborne Rd South SO17 44 D4
Oslo Twrs SO19 59 F6
Osprey Cl, Marchwood SO40 56 C5
Osprey Cl, Southampton SO16 29 F5
Osterley Cl SO30 48 A5
Osterley Rd SO19 59 F1
Otter Cl SO50 23 E6

Otterbourne Hill SO21 13 H5
Otterbourne House Gdns SO21 14 A3
Otterbourne Rd SO21 6 B6
Ouse Cl SO53 12 B6
Outer Circle SO16 29 E6
Outlands La SO30 49 F6
Overbrook SO45 67 E4
Overbrook Way SO52 18 D3
Overcliff Rise SO16 30 A6
Oviat Cl SO40 40 C5
Ovington Rd SO50 31 G1
Owen Rd SO50 21 G6
Oxburgh Cl SO50 21 G3
Oxford Av SO14 5 E1
Oxford Mews SO14 5 E5
Oxford Rd SO14 44 B4
Oxford St SO14 5 E5
Oxlease Cl SO51 9 G4
Ozier Rd SO18 45 H2

Pacific Cl SO14 58 D4
Packridge La SO16 18 C6
Padwell Rd SO14 44 B5
Page Cl SO45 70 C2
Paget St SO14 5 G4
Paignton Rd SO16 42 D3
Paimpol Pl SO51 17 F1
Pallet Cl SO21 15 E5
Pallot Cl SO31 61 E5
Palm Rd SO16 42 D1
Palmers Cl SO50 24 A6
Palmerston Rd SO14 5 F2
Palmerston St SO51 17 F1
Pangbourne Cl SO19 59 F2
Pansy Rd SO16 30 C6
Pantheon Rd SO53 13 G6
Panwell Rd SO18 45 H5
Paradise La, Waltham Chase SO32 37 E4
Paradise La, Woodlands SO40 53 F3
Pardoe Cl SO30 47 G6
Parham Ct SO50 21 G4
Parham Dr SO50 21 G3
Park Cl, Marchwood SO40 56 B5
Park La, Holbury SO45 68 C3
Park La, Marchwood SO40 56 A4
Park La, Otterbourne SO21,50 14 A5
Park La, Southampton SO15 4 C1
Park La, Swanmore SO32 37 H2
Park La, Winchester SO21 7 E6
Park Rd, Bishops Waltham SO32 36 A2
Park Rd, Eastleigh SO53 12 D5
Park Rd, Southampton SO15 43 G6
Park St SO16 43 F4
Park Vw, Botley SO30 48 C5
Park Vw, Hedge End SO30 47 G5
Park Vw, Winchester SO21 6 D5
Park Walk SO14 4 D2
Park Way SO50 24 A5
Parkhill Cl SO45 70 B1
Parklands, Southampton SO18 45 F3
Parklands, Totton SO40 41 G4
Parklands Cl SO53 20 D1
Parkside SO40 55 G1
Parkside Av SO16 42 B4
Parkville Rd SO16 31 E6
Parkway Gdns SO21 21 E1
Parkwood Cl SO30 47 H4
Parnell Rd SO50 21 G6
Parry Rd SO19 60 B2
Parsonage La SO32 34 D4
Parsonage Rd SO14 5 G1
Partridge Rd SO45 67 F5
Partry Cl SO53 12 B6
Passfield Av SO50 21 G5
Passfield Cl SO50 21 F5
Pat Bear Cl SO15 42 A4
Patricia Cl SO30 46 C2
Patricia Dr SO30 47 H5
Paulet Cl SO50 21 H1
Paulet Lacave Av SO16 28 B4
Pauletts La SO40 26 C6
Paulson Cl SO53 12 D6
Pauncefoot Hill SO51 16 C3
Pavilion Cl SO50 33 H1
Pavilion Rd SO30 48 A4
Paxton Cl SO30 48 A6
Paynes La SO50 23 G5
Paynes Rd SO15 43 F6
Peach Rd SO16 29 E6
Peak Cl SO16 42 D4

Pear Tree Cl SO32 48 B2
Pearson La SO21 6 C4
Peartree Av SO19 45 G6
Peartree Cl SO19 59 E2
Peartree Gdns SO18 45 G5
Peartree Rd,
  Dibden Purlieu SO45 67 E4
Peartree Rd,
  Southampton SO19 59 E2
Pebble Ct SO40 56 D4
Peel Cl SO45 10 A4
Peel St SO14 5 G2
Peewit Hill SO31 61 F2
Peewit Hill Cl SO31 61 F2
Pegasus Cl SO31 65 F6
Pegasus Ct SO16 28 D6
Pembers Cl SO50 24 A6
Pembrey Cl SO16 28 D5
Pembroke Cl,
  Eastleigh SO50 21 G2
Pembroke Cl,
  Romsey SO51 9 F6
Pembroke Rd,
  Southampton SO40 41 G3
Pembroke Rd SO19 59 H1
Pendle Cl SO16 42 D4
Pendleton Gdns SO45 70 D3
Pendula Way SO30 22 D3
Penelope Gdns SO31 61 E4
Penfords Pad SO32 36 D3
Penhale Way SO40 41 G5
Penistone Cl SO19 60 A4
Pennard Way SO53 20 B3
Pennine Gdns SO45 66 C4
Pennine Rd SO16 42 C4
Pennine Way SO53 21 E3
Pennington Cl SO21 14 D5
Penrhyn Cl SO50 21 G3
Penshurst Way SO50 21 H1
Pentire Av SO15 43 H2
Pentire Way SO15 43 G2
Pentland Cl SO45 66 C5
Penton Rd SO21 7 F4
Pentridge Way SO40 55 E1
Peppard Cl SO18 45 H5
Peppercorn Way SO30 47 G1
Pepys Av SO19 46 C6
Percivale Rd SO53 20 B3
Percy Cl SO45 67 E1
Percy Rd SO16 43 E4
Peregrine Cl SO40 40 D6
Pern Dr SO30 48 C5
Perran Rd SO16 42 B3
Perryvale Rd SO53 20 B3
Perrywood Cl SO45 70 B1
Perrywood Gdns SO40 40 C4
Peterborough Rd SO14 44 C5
Peterscroft Av SO40 54 B5
Pettinger Gdns SO17 45 E4
Petty Cl SO51 17 G1
Petworth Gdns,
  Eastleigh SO50 21 H2
Petworth Gdns,
  Southampton SO16 29 F5
Pevensey Cl SO16 42 B3
Peverells Rd SO53 21 F1
Peverells Wood Av
  SO53 21 F1
Peverells Wood Cl
  SO53 21 G1
Peveril Rd SO19 59 F2
Pewsey Pl SO15 43 H1
Phillimore Rd SO16 31 E5
Phillips Cl SO16 28 B4
Philpott Dr SO40 56 D5
Phoenix Cl SO31 61 E4
Pickwick Cl SO40 40 B5
Pilands Wood Rd SO31 61 E6
Pilgrim Pl SO18 31 F5
Pilgrims Cl SO53 20 B3
Pine Cl, Ashurst SO40 54 C3
Pine Cl,
  Dibden Purlieu SO45 67 E5
Pine Cl,
  North Baddesley
  SO52 18 D3
Pine Cres SO53 13 E5
Pine Cl SO53 12 D5
Pine Dr SO18 46 C5
Pine Rd,
  Eastleigh SO53 12 C5
Pine Rd, Romsey SO51 18 A1
Pine Rd,
  Southampton SO32 36 D2
Pine Walk SO16 30 A2
Pine Way SO16 30 B2
Pinefield Rd SO18 45 G1
Pinegrove Rd SO19 59 G3
Pinehurst Rd SO16 30 A3
Pinelands Rd SO16 30 A2
Pineview Cl SO31 61 E5
Pinewood SO16 30 B3
Pinewood Cl SO51 10 A4
Pinewood Cres SO45 67 G5
Pinewood Dr SO45 67 G5
Pinewood Pk SO19 61 E1

Pipers Cl SO40 41 E6
Piping Cl SO40 15 E6
Piping Grn SO40 15 E6
Piping Rd SO21 15 E6
Pirelli St SO14 4 C3
Pirrie Cl SO15 43 G3
Pitmore Cl SO16 14 A5
Pitmore Rd SO50 14 A5
Pitt Rd SO15 43 G6
Place La SO21 6 C3
Plaitford Walk SO16 42 D2
Plantation Dr SO40 56 C5
Platform Rd SO14 5 E6
Players Cres SO40 41 F6
Plover Cl SO16 29 E4
Plover Rd SO40 40 D5
Pluto Rd SO50 21 G5
Pointout Cl SO16 43 H1
Pointout Rd SO16 30 A6
Poles La SO21 13 H1
Polesden Cl SO53 12 C5
Pollards Moor Rd
  SO40 38 D6
Polygon Ct SO15 4 C1
Pond Cl SO40 56 D4
Pondhead Cl SO45 70 B1
Pondside La SO32 36 B2
Pooks Grn SO40 56 A4
Poole Rd SO19 59 F2
Popes La, Totton SO40 41 F5
Popes La,
  Upham SO32 25 E3
Poplar Dr SO40 56 B5
Poplar Rd SO19 45 G6
Poplar Way,
  Hedge End SO30 47 H5
Poplar Way,
  North Baddesley
  SO52 18 D2
Poppy Rd SO16 30 D5
Poppyfields SO53 20 B1
Porchester Rd SO19 59 F3
Porlock Rd SO16 42 A3
Portal Rd,
  Eastleigh SO50 22 C4
Portal Rd,
  Southampton SO19 60 A2
Portal Rd, Totton SO40 41 E5
Portchester Rise SO19 21 H1
Portelet Pl SO30 61 H1
Porteous Cres SO53 21 G2
Porters La SO14 4 D6
Portersbridge St SO51 9 E6
Portland St SO14 4 D3
Portland Ter SO14 4 D2
Portside Cl SO40 57 E3
Portsmouth Rd,
  Bursledon SO31 61 E5
Portsmouth Rd,
  Fishers Pond SO50 23 G1
Portsmouth Rd,
  Southampton SO19 59 E3
Portsmouth Rd,
  Upham SO32 25 E4
Portswood Av SO17 44 C3
Portswood Pk SO17 44 C4
Portswood Rd SO17 44 C4
Portview Rd SO18 45 G2
Portway Cl SO18 46 A5
Potters Heron Cl SO51 11 H3
Potters Heron La SO51 11 H3
Poulner Cl SO19 59 H5
Pound La,
  Copythorne SO40 39 E4
Pound La,
  Romsey SO51 11 F3
Pound La, Totton SO40 55 E2
Pound Rd SO31 60 D5
Pound St SO18 45 H5
Pound Tree Rd SO14 4 D3
Powell Cres SO40 55 F1
Precosa Rd SO30 48 A6
Premier Par SO18 45 G1
Premier Way SO51 18 B2
Preshaw Cl SO16 29 F6
Prestwood Rd SO30 47 H6
Pretoria Rd SO31 51 E4
Pricketts Hill SO32 51 E4
Priestcroft Dr SO45 70 D2
Priestlands SO51 9 E5
Priestlands Cl SO40 40 A5
Priestley Cl SO40 40 D5
Priestwood Cl SO16 46 C5
Primrose Cl,
  Eastleigh SO53 20 A3
Primrose Cl,
  Southampton SO16 61 G1
Primrose Rd SO16 30 C5
Primrose Way SO51 9 F6
**Prince Charles Container
Terminal** SO14 56 C1
Prince of Wales Av
  SO15 42 D5
Prince Cl SO16 28 C3
Prince William St SO50 23 E6
Princes Cl SO32 36 A2
Princes Ct SO14 5 G1

Princes Rd SO51 9 E6
Princes St SO14 44 D6
Princess Cl SO30 46 D2
Princess Rd SO40 54 C4
Priors Hill La SO31 60 D6
Priory Av SO17 45 E3
Priory Cl,
  Bishops Waltham
  SO32 36 B2
Priory Cl,
  Southampton SO17 45 E3
Priory Rd,
  Eastleigh SO50 31 G1
Priory Rd, Netley SO31 64 B2
Priory Rd,
  Southampton SO17 44 D4
Proctor Cl SO19 60 C1
Proctor Dr SO52 18 D4
Prospect Pl,
  Eastleigh SO53 20 D1
Prospect Pl,
  Southampton SO45 67 F2
Provene Cl SO32 36 D6
Provene Gdns SO32 36 D6
Providence Hill SO31 61 E6
Prunus Cl SO16 29 G5
Pudbrooke Gdns SO30 47 F4
Pundle Grn SO40 53 E3
Purbrook Cl SO16 29 F5
Purcell Rd SO19 60 B2
Purkess Cl SO53 21 E1
Purkiss Cl SO40 53 F4
Purvis Gdns SO19 60 A4
Pycroft Cl SO19 59 G1
Pylands La SO31 61 F3
Pylewell Rd SO45 71 G1

Quantock Rd SO16 42 C4
Quay Haven SO31 61 H6
Quayside SO30 48 D6
Quayside SO18 45 F5
Quayside Walk SO40 56 D2
Quebec Gdns SO31 61 E5
Queen Cl SO21 7 E6
Queens Cl,
  Romsey SO51 9 G6
Queens Cl,
  Southampton SO45 67 G4
Queens Rd,
  Eastleigh SO53 13 E4
Queens Rd,
  Southampton SO16 43 G2
Queens Ride SO52 18 C4
Queens Ter SO14 5 E5
Queens Vw SO31 64 B2
Queens Way SO14 5 E5
Queenstown Rd SO15 43 G6
Querida Cl SO31 61 H6
Quilter Cl SO19 60 B2
Quob Farm Cl SO30 46 C1
Quob La SO30 32 D6

Rachael Cl SO50 15 F3
Racketts SO45 67 F3
Radcliffe Rd SO14 5 G1
Radleigh Gdns SO40 40 C3
Radstock Rd SO19 59 F3
Radway Cres SO15 43 H3
Radway Rd SO15 43 H4
Raeburn Dr SO30 47 F2
Raglan Cl SO53 20 B4
Railway Cotts SO15 42 A4
Railway View Rd SO17 44 D3
Ralphs La SO31 9 H5
Ramalley La SO53 12 C6
Rampart Rd SO18 45 E4
Randall Cl SO40 40 D1
Randall Rd SO53 13 G4
Randolph St SO15 43 G5
Ranelagh Gdns SO15 44 A5
Ranfurly Gdns SO45 67 E5
Range Gdns SO30 60 A3
Ranmore Cl SO45 66 B3
Rareridge La SO32 36 D1
Ratcliffe Rd,
  Dibden Purlieu SO45 67 F5
Ratcliffe Rd,
  Hedge End SO30 47 G5
Rathdora Mews SO31 61 H6
Rattigan Gdns PO15 63 E6
Raven Rd SO14 5 F1
Raven Sq SO50 21 E6
Ravenscroft Cl SO31 61 E5
Ravenscroft Way SO32 48 B3
Raymond Cl,
  Holbury SO45 70 C1
Raymond Cl,
  West End SO30 47 E1
Raymond Rd SO15 43 H4
Rayners Gdns SO16 31 E6
Reading Room La
  SO32 49 F4
Rectory Cl SO30 48 A6
Red La SO32 24 D2
Red Leaves SO32 50 D1

Red Lion St*,
  Houchin St SO32 36 C2
Red Lodge SO53 20 D5
Redbridge Causeway
  SO40 41 H4
Redbridge Flyover
  SO15 42 A3
Redbridge Hill SO16 42 D3
Redbridge La SO16 28 B6
Redbridge Rd SO15 42 A4
Redbridge Twrs SO16 42 A5
Redcar SO15 43 F3
Redcote Cl SO18 46 A5
Redcroft La SO31 61 F5
Redhill SO16 29 H6
Redhill Cres SO16 29 H6
Redhill Way SO16 29 H6
Redlands Dr SO19 45 G6
Redmoor Cl SO19 45 G6
Redrise Cl SO45 70 A1
Redward Rd SO16 28 C5
Redwing Gdns SO40 40 C4
Redwood Cl,
  West End SO30 46 B1
Redwood Cl SO16 30 B4
Redwood Gdns SO40 40 D5
Redwood Way SO16 30 B4
Reed Dr SO40 56 D4
Reeves Rowland Ct
  SO30 48 C5
Reeves Way SO31 61 E5
Regent Cl SO21 14 B2
Regent Ct SO17 44 B3
Regent Rd SO21 21 E2
Regent St SO14 4 D3
Regents Gro SO15 43 F3
Regents Park Gdns
  SO15 43 E4
Regents Park Rd SO15 43 E6
Reliant Cl SO53 20 C3
Renda Rd SO45 68 D6
Renown Cl SO53 20 C3
Repton Gdns SO30 47 H2
Reservoir La SO30 47 F6
Retail Village SO15 58 A2
Rex Ind Est SO53 21 E2
Reynolds Cl SO15 17 H1
Reynolds Dale SO40 54 D1
Reynolds Rd,
  Eastleigh SO50 23 H6
Reynolds Rd,
  Southampton SO15 43 G4
Rhinefield Cl SO30 22 D5
Rhyme Hall Mews
  SO45 71 G1
Ribble Cl SO53 21 E2
Ribble Cl SO16 42 C3
Richard Taunton Pl
  SO17 44 B1
Richards Cl SO45 71 E2
Richards Cl SO30 46 B2
Richlans Rd SO30 47 G6
Richmond Cl,
  Eastleigh SO53 12 D4
Richmond Cl,
  Southampton SO40 40 C2
Richmond Gdns SO17 44 D2
Richmond La SO51 9 G4
Richmond Pk SO21 14 C1
Richmond Rd SO15 43 F6
Richmond St SO14 5 F5
Richville Rd SO16 43 E4
Ridding Cl SO15 43 F3
Ridge La,
  Romsey SO51 16 B6
Ridge La,
  Southampton SO30 63 F2
Ridgemount Av SO16 30 A4
Ridgemount La SO16 30 A4
Ridgeway Cl,
  Chandlers Ford SO53 21 F3
Ridgeway Cl,
  Fair Oak SO50 23 G4
Ridgeway Walk SO53 21 F3
Ridgewood Cl SO45 66 B3
Ridley Cl SO40 70 B1
Rigby Rd SO17 44 C4
Rimington Gdns SO51 9 H4
Ringwood Dr SO52 18 C3
Ringwood Rd SO40 40 A5
Ripon Ct SO50 34 A3
Ripplewood SO40 57 E4
Ripstone Gdns SO17 44 C1
Ritchie Ct SO19 60 A2
River Grn SO31 72 C1
River View Rd SO18 45 E2
River Walk SO18 45 F1
Riverdene Pl SO18 45 F3
Rivermead Cl SO51 16 D1
Riversdale Cl SO19 59 F6
Riverside SO50 23 G4
Riverside SO18 45 F4
Riverside Cl SO18 45 F4
Riverside Gdns SO51 17 E1

Riverside Mews PO17 72 D5
Riverview SO40 55 F1
Riverview Ter SO31 62 A6
Robert Cecil Av SO18 31 F6
Robert Whitworth Dr
  SO51 9 F5
Roberts Cl PO17 72 C5
Roberts Rd,
  Hythe SO45 67 E2
Roberts Rd,
  Southampton SO15 4 A1
Roberts Rd,
  Totton SO40 41 F6
Robin Gdns SO40 40 C4
Robin Sq SO50 21 E6
Robinia Grn SO16 29 G5
Robson Cl SO45 70 B1
Rochester St SO14 5 G2
Rockall Cl SO16 28 C5
Rockery Cl SO45 66 C3
Rockleigh Dr SO40 55 E1
Rockleigh Rd SO16 43 H1
Rockram Cl SO40 53 E2
Rockram Gdns SO45 66 B3
Rockstone La SO14 44 B5
Rockstone Pl SO15 44 B5
Roewood Cl SO45 70 B1
Roewood Rd SO45 70 B1
Rogers Cl SO50 22 C3
Rogers Rd SO50 22 D3
Roker Way SO50 33 G1
Rollestone Rd SO45 70 A1
Roman Cl SO53 21 F1
Roman Dr SO16 30 A3
Roman Gdns SO45 66 C5
Roman Rd,
  Chilworth SO16 29 H1
Roman Rd,
  Dibden Purlieu SO45 66 C5
Roman Rd,
  Winchester SO21 7 F6
Roman Row SO32 36 C2
Roman Rd SO14 4 D4
Roman Way SO45 66 C5
Romill Cl SO18 32 A6
Romsey By-Pass SO51 17 E2
Romsey Cl SO51 21 H5
Romsey Ind Est SO51 9 F5
Romsey Rd,
  Cadnam SO40 38 C6
Romsey Rd,
  Eastleigh SO50 21 H5
Romsey Rd,
  Romsey SO51 39 H1
Romsey Rd,
  Southampton SO16 28 A1
Rookley SO31 64 C1
Rooksbridge SO45 66 B3
Rookwood Cl SO50 21 H1
Ropewalk SO31 65 G6
Ropley Cl SO19 59 H6
Rose Cl,
  Hedge End SO30 47 G3
Rose Cl, Hythe SO45 67 F5
Rose Rd,
  Southampton SO14 44 B4
Rose Rd, Totton SO40 41 G6
Rosebank Cl SO16 28 C4
Rosebery Av SO45 67 G5
Rosebery Cres SO50 22 A2
Rosedale Av SO51 17 G1
Rosehip Cl SO30 23 F6
Roselands SO30 46 C4
Roselands Cl SO50 23 G5
Roselands Gdns SO17 44 C2
Roseleigh Dr SO40 41 E6
Rosemary Cl SO40 40 C4
Rosemary Gdns,
  Fareham PO15 63 F6
Rosemary Gdns,
  Southampton SO30 61 G1
Rosemary Price Ct
  SO30 47 G4
Rosemoor Ct SO53 12 C5
Rosendale Rd SO53 21 E3
Rosewall Rd SO16 42 D1
Rosewood Gdns SO40 57 E5
Rosoman Rd SO19 59 G2
Ross Gdns SO16 43 E2
Ross Mews SO31 64 A2
Rossington Av SO18 45 G4
Rossington Way SO18 45 G4
Rossiters La SO50 53 G4
Rosslyn Cl SO52 18 D3
Rostron Cl SO18 45 H1
Rosyth Rd SO18 45 G4
Rotary Ct SO31 64 B2
Rothbury Cl,
  Southampton SO19 59 H2
Rothbury Cl,
  Totton SO40 41 E3
Rother Cl SO18 46 A3
Rother Dale SO19 60 C2
Rothsbury Dr SO53 20 C2
Rothschild Cl SO19 59 F5
Rothville Pl SO53 12 C3
Rotterdam Twrs SO19 59 G6

82

Eastleigh SO53 20 B2
The Meads,
　Romsey SO51 16 D1
The Mews,
　Eastleigh SO53 20 D5
The Mews,
　Southampton SO16 28 C3
The Mews*,
　Lepe Rd SO53 70 D5
The Mill Pond SO45 68 C4
The Mount,
　Shirley Park SO16 43 E3
The Mount,
　Southampton SO16 30 A6
The Nook SO50 22 A3
The Oaklands SO53 20 D5
The Oaks,
　Bursledon SO31 61 E6
The Oaks,
　Southampton SO19 59 G1
The Old Well Cl SO19 60 A3
The Orchard,
　Bassett Green SO16 30 C5
The Orchard,
　Chilworth SO16 30 A1
The Paddock,
　Eastleigh SO50 22 A1
The Paddock,
　Southampton SO40 40 D2
The Paddocks SO45 71 F1
The Parade SO40 52 C1
The Parkway SO16 30 C5
The Pentagon SO45 71 E2
The Pines SO16 43 F1
The Plantation SO32 49 G2
The Polygon SO15 4 C1
The Poplars SO32 50 D1
The Precinct SO45 68 D6
The Premier Centre
　SO51 18 B2
The Priory SO32 36 B2
The Promenade SO45 67 G2
The Quadrangle,
　Eastleigh SO50 21 H4
The Quadrangle,
　Romsey SO51 18 B2
The Quantocks SO34 66 D4
The Recess SO50 22 A3
The Redfords SO40 41 E3
The Retreat,
　Eastleigh SO50 22 A4
The Retreat,
　Southampton SO40 55 G1
The Ridings,
　Eastleigh SO50 23 F5
The Ridings,
　Southampton SO32 37 E6
The Ring SO16 30 A3
The Rowans SO40 56 C5
The Rushes SO40 56 D4
The Saplings SO45 68 D5
The Sawmills SO32 34 D5
The Shires SO30 47 F6
The Siblings SO19 44 D6
The Sidings SO31 64 D3
The Sidings Ind Est
　SO31 64 C3
The Spinney,
　Calmore SO40 40 C3
The Spinney,
　Eastleigh SO50 23 F5
The Spinney,
　Southampton SO16 30 B3
The Spinney,
　Winchester SO21 6 B5
The Spur PO17 72 C4
The Square,
　Fareham PO17 72 C5
The Square,
　Fawley SO45 71 G1
The Square,
　Hamble SO31 65 G6
The Straight Mile
　SO51 10 C4
The Swan Centre
　SO50 21 H5
The Sylvans SO45 66 C4
The Tanyards SO15 12 C5
The Thicket SO51 18 A2
The Tower Ind Est
　SO50 22 A6
The Triangle SO18 45 F3
The Triton Centre SO51 18 B2
The Tussocks SO40 56 D4
The Tyleshades SO51 17 G1
The Vale SO45 67 E4
The Vikings SO51 18 A1
The Vineyards SO52 19 E3
The Warren SO45 68 C5
The Westering SO51 10 A5
The Wicket SO45 67 E4
The Willows SO30 46 D1
The Willows*,
　Nursery Gdns SO53 20 D5
Thetford Gdns SO53 12 B6
Third Av SO15 42 C5
Third St SO45 69 G6

Thirlmere SO50 21 G6
Thirlmere Rd SO16 42 C1
Thirlstane Firs SO53 20 C4
Thirteenth St SO45 69 E5
Thistle Rd,
　Eastleigh SO53 20 A3
Thistle Rd,
　Southampton SO30 47 F5
Thomas Cl SO40 40 D5
Thomas Lewis Way
　SO16 31 E6
Thomas Rd SO52 19 E4
Thompsons La SO50 24 A1
Thorn Cl SO50 21 H3
Thornbury Av,
　Blackfield SO45 70 D4
Thornbury Av,
　Southampton SO15 43 H4
Thornbury Heights
　SO53 13 G5
Thornbury Wood SO53 13 G5
Thorndike Cl SO16 42 D1
Thorndike Rd SO16 42 D2
Thorness Cl SO16 42 A2
Thorneycroft Av SO19 59 F4
Thornhill Av SO19 46 C5
Thornhill Cl SO45 71 E3
Thornhill Park Rd
　SO18 46 B5
Thornhill Rd,
　Blackfield SO45 71 E2
Thornhill Rd,
　Southampton SO16 29 H6
Thornleigh Rd SO19 59 F3
Thorold Rd,
　Eastleigh SO53 13 F5
Thorold Rd,
　Southampton SO18 45 F3
Three Oaks SO19 60 D1
Threefield La SO14 5 E5
Thruxton Ct SO19 59 F1
Thurmell Cl SO30 61 G2
Thurmell Walk SO30 61 H2
Thurston Cl SO53 13 E6
Thyme Av PO15 63 F6
Tichborne Rd,
　Eastleigh SO50 31 G1
Tichborne Rd,
　Southampton SO18 46 C4
Tickleford Dr SO19 59 H6
Tickner Cl SO30 62 A1
Ticonderoga Gdns
　SO19 59 F5
Tides Reach SO18 45 E4
Tides Way SO40 56 D3
Tilbrook Rd SO15 43 E4
Tilden Rd SO21 6 B6
Timberley Cl SO45 68 D6
Timor Cl PO15 63 E5
Timothy Cl SO15 4 A1
Timsbury Dr SO16 42 D2
Timson Cl SO40 40 D5
Tindale Rd SO16 42 C2
Tinker Alley SO18 31 H3
Tintagel Cl SO16 42 C2
Tintern Gro SO15 4 B1
Tiptree Cl SO60 21 H3
Titchfield La PO17 72 A6
Tithewood Cl SO53 12 C4
Tivoli Cl SO53 13 G6
Tolefrey Gdns SO53 20 A1
Tollbar Way SO30 33 G6
Tollgate SO53 20 D6
Tollgate Rd SO31 61 H6
Tommy Green Walk
　SO50 21 G5
Toogoods Way SO30 28 B5
Toomer Cl SO45 71 E2
Toothill Rd SO51 18 A6
Torch Cl SO30 23 F5
Torcross Cl SO19 59 G4
Tormead SO45 67 E4
Tornay Gro SO52 18 C4
Torquay Av SO15 43 G4
Torque Cl SO19 60 D2
Torre Cl SO50 21 H1
Torridge Gdns SO18 46 A1
Torrington Cl SO19 59 H2
Torwood Gdns SO50 23 E5
Tosson Cl SO16 42 C4
Totland Cl SO16 42 B3
Totnes Cl SO50 21 G2
Tottehale Cl SO52 18 D4
Totton SO40 41 G5
Totton Western By-Pass
　SO51 26 A5
Tower Gdns SO16 30 A6
Tower La SO50 22 A6
Tower Pl SO30 46 C3
Town Quay SO14 4 D5
Townhill Way SO18 45 H1
Toynbee Cl SO50 21 H4
Toynbee Rd SO50 21 H5
Trafalgar Cl SO53 20 C2
Trafalgar Rd SO15 43 F5
Trafalgar Way SO45 67 G5
Trafford Rd SO18 33 G1

Tranby Rd SO19 59 F2
Treagore Rd SO40 40 D3
Trearnan Cl SO16 42 D3
Treeside Av SO40 41 G5
Treeside Rd SO15 43 G4
Treloyhan Cl SO53 21 E3
Tremona Cl SO16 43 F2
Tremona Rd SO16 43 F1
Trenley Cl SO45 70 B1
Trent Cl SO18 45 G3
Trent Rd SO18 45 G3
Trent Way SO30 46 A1
Tresillian Gdns SO18 46 A1
Trevone Cl SO40 55 E1
Trevose Cl SO53 21 E3
Trevose Cres SO53 21 E3
Triangle Gdns SO16 28 B6
Trinity Ct,
　Eastleigh SO53 21 E1
Trinity Ct,
　Southampton SO40 41 F2
Trinity Ind Est SO15 42 C5
Trinity Rd SO14 5 E2
Tristram Cl SO53 20 B3
Trotts La SO40 56 A2
Trowbridge Cl SO16 28 C4
Truro Rise SO50 21 H2
Tudor Cl SO40 40 C3
Tudor Gdns SO30 61 F1
Tudor Wood Cl SO16 30 A6
Tuffin Cl SO16 28 C4
Tulip Rd SO16 30 D6
Tumulus Cl SO19 60 C2
Tunstall Rd SO19 60 C2
Turnpike Way SO30 47 F4
Turnstone Gdns SO16 29 E5
Tuscan Walk SO53 21 F1
Tutland Rd SO52 18 D3
Tutor Cl SO31 65 E5
Tweed Cl SO53 12 B6
Twelfth St SO45 69 E5
Twiggs La SO40 56 C6
Twyford Av SO15 43 G3
Twyford Rd,
　Eastleigh SO50 22 A1
Twyford Rd,
　Winchester SO21 7 E2
Twynhams Hill SO32 51 F3
Tyne Cl SO53 20 C3
Tyne Way SO30 46 C2
Tyrrel Rd SO30 13 E6
Tytherley Rd SO18 46 B4

Ullswater SO50 21 H6
Ullswater Av SO16 46 A3
Ullswater Rd SO16 42 C2
Undercliff Gdns SO30 30 A6
Underwood Cl SO16 30 A6
Underwood Rd,
　Eastleigh SO50 22 C4
Underwood Rd,
　Southampton SO16 30 A6
Union Rd SO14 44 D6
University Cres SO17 30 C6
University Parkway
　SO16 19 H6
University Rd SO17 30 C6
Unwin Cl SO19 59 E5
Upham St SO32 25 E4
Uplands Way SO17 44 C2
Upmill Cl SO30 46 A1
Upper Banister St
　SO15 44 B6
Upper Barn Copse
　SO50 23 G4
Upper Brownhill Rd
　SO16 28 C6
Upper Bugle St SO14 4 D4
Upper Church Rd SO32 51 E5
Upper Crescent Rd
　SO52 18 D3
Upper Deacon Rd
　SO19 46 A6
Upper House Cte PO17 72 C5
Upper Mead Cl SO50 23 H6
Upper Moors Rd SO50 14 D6
Upper Mullins La SO45 67 E4
Upper New Rd SO30 46 C3
Upper Northam Cl
　SO30 47 E6
Upper Northam Dr
　SO30 46 D5
Upper Northam Rd
　SO30 47 E5
Upper St Helens Rd
　SO30 61 G2
Upper Shaftesbury Av
　SO17 44 D2
Upper Shirley Av
　SO15 43 G3
Upper Toothill Rd
　SO16 28 C1
Upper Weston La
　SO19 59 H4
Upper Yardley Rd
　SO30 59 G1
Upton Cres SO16 28 A3

Upton La SO16 27 G4
Vale Dr SO18 45 G3
Valentine Av SO19 60 B3
Valerian Cl SO50 33 H3
Valerian Rd SO30 47 H6
Valley Cl,
　Southampton SO45 70 D3
Valley Cl,
　Winchester SO21 15 E6
Valley Rd,
　Eastleigh SO53 12 D6
Valley Rd,
　Southampton SO40 55 F1
Valleydene SO45 67 F5
Vanburgh Way SO53 12 C4
Vanguard Rd SO18 45 H3
Vardy Cl SO19 60 C3
Varna Rd SO15 43 G6
Vaudrey Cl SO15 43 F3
Vaughan Cl SO19 60 D1
Vaughan Rd SO45 66 C3
Vears La SO21 15 E5
Vellan Ct SO16 42 A3
Velmore Rd SO53 20 C4
Velsheda Ct SO45 67 F1
Ventnor Ct SO16 30 D5
Venture Rd SO16 29 G1
Verbena Way SO30 47 H6
Verdon Av SO31 65 E5
Vermont Cl SO16 30 A5
Verona Rd SO53 21 F1
Verulam Rd SO14 44 C4
Vespasian Rd SO18 45 E4
Vespasian Way SO53 21 F1
Vesta Way SO30 13 F6
Vicarage Dr SO30 61 F1
Vicarage La,
　Copythorne SO40 39 E6
Vicarage La,
　Curdridge SO32 49 E4
Vicarage La,
　Swanmore SO32 37 H4
Vicarage Rd SO40 56 D5
Viceroy Rd SO19 59 H3
Victena Rd SO50 23 G5
Victor St SO15 43 F3
Victoria Pl SO51 9 F6
Victoria Rd,
　Bishops Waltham
　SO32 36 B2
Victoria Rd,
　Eastleigh SO50 22 A2
Victoria Rd,
　Netley SO31 64 A2
Victoria Rd,
　Southampton SO19 59 E5
Victoria St SO14 5 G2
Victoria Walk SO30 46 D1
Victory Cl SO53 20 C3
Victory Cres SO15 43 F5
Victory Rd SO15 43 F5
Victory Sq SO15 43 F5
Victory Way SO16 28 C3
Viking Cl,
　Blackfield SO45 71 E4
Viking Cl,
　Southampton SO16 28 C5
Villiers Rd,
　Dibden Purlieu SO45 67 E6
Villiers Rd,
　Southampton SO15 43 F4
Vincent Av SO16 43 G2
Vincent Gro SO15 43 F4
Vincent St SO15 43 F3
Vincents Walk SO14 4 D3
Vine Bank SO18 46 A3
Vine Rd SO16 43 E1
Vinery Gdns SO53 43 F2
Vinery Rd SO16 43 F2
Viney Av SO51 9 H5
Vineyard Cl SO19 59 E3
Violet Cl SO53 20 B1
Violet Rd SO16 30 B5
Vokes Cl SO19 60 A1
Vulcan Cl SO15 42 D5
Vulcan Rd SO15 42 D5
Vyse La SO14 4 D5

Wade Hill Dro SO40 26 C4
Wadhurst Gdns SO19 59 H6
Wadhurst Rd SO30 47 G6
Wadmore Cl SO45 67 G2
Wainwright Gdns
　SO30 47 G1
Wakefield Cl SO18 45 H3
Wakefield Rd SO18 45 H3
Waldegrave Cl SO19 59 E5
Waldon Gdns SO30 46 A1
Walker Gdns SO30 47 H3
Walkers Cl SO50 24 A6
Walkers La North
　SO45 70 D3
Walkers La South
　SO45 71 E5
Wallace Rd SO19 59 G5
Wallington Dr SO53 12 C5

Walmer Cl SO50 21 H1
Walnut Av SO18 31 F5
Walnut Cl,
　Eastleigh SO53 12 D4
Walnut Cl,
　Southampton SO16 42 D3
Walnut Gro SO16 42 D3
Walpole La SO31 62 A6
Walsingham Gdns
　SO18 45 G1
Waltham Cres SO16 29 F5
Walton Rd SO19 60 D2
Waltons Av SO45 69 E6
Wangfield La SO32 48 D2
Wansbeck Cl SO53 20 C2
Warbler Cl SO16 29 F4
Warblington Cl SO53 20 C4
Warburton Cl SO19 60 D2
Warburton Rd SO19 60 C1
Warden Cl SO30 46 C3
Wardle Rd SO50 14 C6
Warlock Cl SO19 60 C2
Warner Mews SO30 48 C5
Warren Av,
　Eastleigh SO53 21 F3
Warren Av,
　Southampton SO16 43 E1
Warren Cl,
　Eastleigh SO53 21 F2
Warren Cl,
　Southampton SO16 43 E2
Warren Cres SO16 43 E2
Warren Gdns SO51 9 H4
Warren Pl SO40 40 D2
Warrior Cl SO53 20 D3
Warrys Cl SO45 68 B2
Warwick Cl SO53 20 C3
Warwick Rd,
　Southampton SO15 43 H2
Warwick Rd,
　Totton SO40 41 F3
Warwick Way PO17 72 C5
Water La,
　Dibden Purlieu SO45 66 D5
Water La,
　Southampton SO15 4 C1
Water La, Totton SO40 40 D4
Waterbeech Dr SO30 47 G4
Waterhouse La SO15 43 E5
Waterhouse Way SO15 43 E5
Waterloo Ind Est
　SO30 47 F3
Waterloo Rd SO15 4 A1
Waterloo Ter SO15 4 D1
Watermans La SO45 67 E6
Waters Edge SO30 47 F6
Waterside SO45 67 F1
Waterside Rd SO51 9 G4
Waterside Sq*,
　Waterside SO45 67 F1
Waterworks Rd SO21 14 B1
Watkin Rd SO30 47 H2
Watley Cl SO16 42 B3
Watley Cl SO21 7 G5
Watson Walk SO40 40 C5
Watton Rd SO45 70 B1
Watts Cl SO16 42 C1
Watts Rd SO30 47 G5
Wavecrest Cl SO40 56 D3
Wavell Rd SO18 45 G3
Waveney Grn SO16 42 C3
Waverley Av SO31 64 C2
Waverley Cl SO51 9 H5
Waverley Rd SO15 43 C3
Waverley Rd SO15 4 A2
Waylands Pl SO30 61 F2
Waynflete Cl SO32 36 B1
Wayside SO31 61 H6
Weardale Rd SO53 21 E3
Weavers Pl SO53 12 C5
Weavills Rd SO50 23 E6
Webburn Gdns SO18 45 H1
Wedgewood Cl SO45 68 D6
Welbeck Av SO17 44 C1
Welch Way SO16 28 C5
Well La, Hamble SO31 65 H5
Well La,
　Swanmore SO32 37 H3
Welland Gdns SO18 46 A2
Welland Grn SO16 42 C3
Wellbrooke Gdns
　SO53 12 C6
Wellers Cl SO40 40 B5
Welles Rd SO53 21 E1
Wellington Av SO18 46 A5
Wellington Cl SO45 66 D5
Wellington Pk SO30 47 F3
Wellington Pl SO40 52 C1
Wellington Rd SO18 45 F2
Wellow Cl SO18 46 A5
Wellowbrook Cl SO53 20 C2
Wells Cl PO15 63 E5
Wells Pl SO50 21 H5
Welshers La SO21 6 B4
Wembley Way SO50 15 G6
Wentworth Gdns,